THROUGH THE EYES OF THEIR CHILDREN

Myron H. Fox

■

DORIS MINSKY MEMORIAL FUND

Publication No. 5

PUBLICATION COMMITTEE

Charles B. Bernstein, Chairman and Editor
Irving H. Cutler
Joe Kraus
Walter Roth
Norman D. Schwartz
Irwin J. Suloway

CHICAGO JEWISH HISTORICAL SOCIETY
618 South Michigan Avenue, Chicago, Illinois 60605

The Chicago Jewish Historical Society was founded in 1977 and is in part an outgrowth of local Jewish participation in the American Bicentennial celebrations of 1976. It has as its purpose the discovery, preservation and dissemination of information concerning the Jewish experience in the Chicago area.

Library of Congress Catalog Control Number: 00-131967
ISBN 1-884703-03-8

Printed in the United States of America

Please direct all orders and correspondence to the Publisher at the above address.

Front cover photograph: Bella and Philip Fox at time of their engagement, summer 1923; back cover photograph: Philip Fox at age 61, winter 1962 (both photographs from collection of Myron H. Fox)

DEDICATION

This book is dedicated to the memory

of

my parents,

Philip Fox

and

Bella Leibovitz Fox

CONTENTS

PREFACE

Doris Minsky was a founder, director and officer of the Chicago Jewish Historical Society from its inception to the date of her untimely death. She was completely committed to the many volunteer activities of the Society. One of her great loves was for exhibits picturing the lives of our forefathers in Chicago. The last exhibit she worked on, as I recall, dealt with the life of Samuel Meisenberg, a young Chicago Jewish man who was one of the first U.S. Marines killed in Vera Cruz, Mexico, in April, 1914, during the Mexican War of that year. The Meisenberg exhibit was typical of her many efforts for the Society.

In order to perpetuate her memory, Doris's husband, Joseph Minsky, who subsequently also has passed away, with contributions made by himself, his family and many friends, established the Doris Minsky fund for the purpose of publishing annually monographs dealing with the history of the Jewish people of Chicago. This year, a committee consisting of Charles B. Bernstein, chairman and editor; Irving H. Cutler, Joe Kraus, Walter Roth and Irwin J. Suloway was appointed to screen the many writings that were submitted and to choose winners of the cash prize also awarded by the fund.

The committee has decided that one entry should be awarded first prize this year, and this entry appears as the Fund's fifth publication. The work by Myron H. Fox constitutes a superb continuation for The Doris Minsky Memorial Fund Monographs. The society congratulates the committee and all those who have contributed to the Doris Minsky Fund for making possible this magnificent addition to the history of Chicago's Jews.

Walter Roth
President
Chicago Jewish Historical Society

FOREWORD

This book by a devoted son deals with a murder during Chicago's bloody taxicab war of the 1920s. The author's father was a Checker Cab driver who was arrested, tortured, convicted of murder, and imprisoned for life, and after almost two years of imprisonment, was substantially exonerated by a pardon. It also recounts the eighty-year story of the author's immigrant Jewish family who came from Eastern Europe in 1912 and made their way to Chicago. It is an extraordinary and touching act of filial piety designed to defend the memory of a dead father.

In 1921 at age twenty, Philip Fox, the author's father, was a Checker Cab Company driver-owner during a bitter taxi war between the Yellow Cab Company and Checker. With the aid of a license system obtained from a corrupt city administration, Yellow sought to drive Checker cabs out of business. On the night of June 8, 1921, a dark automobile with five or six passengers drove past a Yellow Cab station firing bullets. A Yellow Cab driver was killed.

Soon after, the police went to a Checker hangout and arrested Philip Fox and another Checker driver-owner. All night long, at intervals, two Yellow Cab lawyers, former Judge George Barrett and Ben Samuels (my erstwhile Sunday School teacher), interrogated the two drivers. From time to time, until "confessions" were obtained, Judge Barrett would tell the police to "take them away," and the police would take them individually to a dark room where the police beat them mercilessly and lied to them extravagantly. Fortunately, the story of that brutal treatment was told and preserved in the dissenting opinion of Illinois Supreme Court Justice Duncan in 319 Illinois 606. At last, both men were forced to confess that they were in the murder car. Philip Fox's confession was repudiated and was so tainted it was never used, but the other driver's confession implicated Philip and was admitted against both of them.

Drawing on what records he could find and oral reports he could elicit, the author tells of Philip's first trial with a hung jury, his second trial and conviction of murder, his futile appeal to the Illinois Supreme Court, his imprisonment in Stateville beginning in January

1926, and his pardon by Governor Len Small in December 1928 as Small's term was expiring.

As to the taxi war, Yellow and Checker resolved it profitably. That is not a part of this story. Both companies came under one ownership, and together they established a lucrative taxicab monopoly which lasted for many years. When Philip Fox came out of prison in 1928, Checker gave him a good job which he performed creditably until retirement.

The author, who was born after his father's pardon, learned about Philip's conviction and imprisonment only years after Philip had died in 1982. He then set about learning all he could from available sources and wrote this book to honor his father and his father's family.

We can be sure that Philip Fox did not kill the Yellow Cab driver on June 8, 1921, because Ben Samuels, the Yellow Cab attorney, ultimately conceded that the fatal bullet came from a .38 caliber revolver and the gun ascribed to Philip Fox was a .32. Was Philip Fox a passenger in the dark automobile that drove past the Yellow Cab station? We will never know for certain. The author presents a convincing case that Philip was innocent.

The book is a valuable addition to a significant chapter of Chicago's history.

Leon M. Despres

THROUGH THE EYES OF THEIR CHILDREN

Myron H. Fox

ACKNOWLEDGMENTS

Writing this book required a lot of time and concentration, and most of all, encouragement, which I received from my wonderful wife, Frances. Her confidence in my ability to do it, and her encouragement for me to go forward whenever I was at an impasse, was the primary ingredient for completion.

Acknowledging everyone who contributed to this work is a pleasure. First I have to thank my sisters, Esther Brutzkus and Helen Fryer, and my brothers, Edward and Morton Fox, whose input was invaluable. I then want to thank my nephew Michael Fryer, an award winning photographer with the *Chicago Tribune*, for his valuable research. I want to thank my cousin Mitchell Kreiter, a prominent Chicago criminal attorney, for obtaining several of the legal documents I have used.

One large thank you to all of the grandchildren of Max and Marion Fox, who allowed me to interview them. Recalling the wonderful stories of the past was a lot of fun. Philip and Bella always loved and respected their nieces and nephews and this feeling was truly mutual.

The interest of my seven children in their background and the story of their grandparents added to the incentive to go ahead with this project. To the seven of them, Sherrie, Elaine, Stacey, Lorin, Norman, Charmaine and Marshall, I say thank you and I love you.

One final huge thank you to my daughter Sherrie, who was my right arm in this project, with her intellect and computer skills.

Myron H. Fox

INTRODUCTION

Due to the seventy-three year silence of our parents, this book had to be written in retrospect. In the late summer of 1975, while my brother Morton and I were visiting with relatives in South Bend, Indiana, a couple of veiled hints were dropped alluding to secrets in the pasts of our parents. I pushed these to the back of my subconscious where they lay dormant for the next twelve years. In 1987, on a trip to California with my wife Frances and my sister Esther, we visited at the home of my mother's cousin. There the second clue was revealed. As soon as she repeated and corroborated the same statements that we had heard in South Bend, I knew that there was a lot more to this story of my parents' past. When, in 1994, I learned for certain of these well kept secrets, I fell upon the task of research. Old files and legal archives surrendered a goodly portion of information, while the microfilm editions of the Chicago daily newspapers produced headlines and stories from the twenties and thirties. Interviewing relatives, I was able to find more pieces to the puzzle. After gathering all the parts, it was then only "through the eyes of their children" that I was able to fit it all together.

This discovery of the early past was the impetus and inspiration to put pen to paper to demonstrate for posterity our love and affection for this husband and wife team who gave us our creation and guidance throughout our lives. Their intention never to reveal their early story to us, though perhaps misguided, was meant for one purpose only, and that was that their children should be protected from any harm because of innuendo or gossip.

When I began this book, I could not have been less aware of the gamut of emotions I would experience by the time of its completion. It has been a catharsis for me and all of my brothers and sisters. We never knew until now all the troubles and travail in the lives of our parents, Philip and Bella Fox, that preceded our existence.

As I write this book in 1995, all of the people who were directly involved or had direct knowledge of what took place in those long-ago days have passed away. From all of the research I have done, I have not been able to locate any one of them still alive. Only my mother, Bella Fox, who celebrated her ninetieth birthday just before I completed the manuscript, could attest to some of these facts.

Searching for material to write this story seventy-five years later became quite a challenge. It was a labor of love to seek and find the truth. My father was totally innocent of the crime of which he was accused and convicted. He served three years in Stateville Penitentiary, suffering the indignities inflicted upon him for a crime he did not commit.

Only through early newspaper accounts from 1921 through 1928 plus transcripts of the Pardon Board and the appeal case in the Illinois Supreme Court, which has become a text book case on the legal issue of "Voluntary and Involuntary Confessions," *People vs. Philip Fox*, 319 Ill. 606, have I been able to piece together with great certainty the truth of this story as I have depicted it in this book. The actual transcripts of the first and second trials have since been destroyed. All that is left is the verdicts and the consequences of them. Well known names in Chicago business and politics wind their way through this story, playing a role through their actions that reverberates upon the lives of people they will never meet.

Although this is a personal account of the lives of our mother and father, it can stand as an inspiration to others. To overcome adversities is not an uncommon act. But to overcome adversities and not fall victim to bitterness and hatred towards the society that inflicted it upon you, requires a greater strength than most people possess. Philip overcame the normal inclination for revenge, and the "get even" mentality that permeates our society. It required great determination and will power to put aside those feelings, and summon all of the positives that he experienced already in his young life. He used those positives as a springboard to the future he thought about and longed for during the period of his incarceration. He never abandoned his ideals for equality amongst men and their right to earn a fair and honest living for themselves and their families. He now knew he could not accomplish these things with his fists and temper.

When the judicial system realized its error and Philip received his full pardon and restoration of his citizenship and rights, he knew from that point forward that he would become an upstanding citizen, and would work towards the betterment of the America that he loved. From the day he emerged from prison to the day that he passed away, a period of over fifty-three years, he never gave any indication that he harbored hatred or disdain for his country or society in general. This almost single-minded devotion to country and the rights of the individual, which had been known to his children, took on a whole new significance later in life with the revelation of our father's past. This was only one of the legacies of inspiration that he bequeathed to his descendants.

Our mother, whose stoic persona belied her courageous youth, was a heroine of a different kind. She learned early in life what it meant to be lonely and afraid, but also to be courageous and resourceful. At age fifteen, forced to adapt to unfamiliar and at times frightening surroundings in a new and strange land, she displayed an uncommon inner strength. For the next twenty years, she suffered through circumstances and events that would challenge most people's faith in both God and man. She never let it happen. Her dignity and faith remained constant throughout the years. Her Jewish Orthodoxy was her guide, and the love of her husband and children and their welfare was the core of her adult life. As busy as she was in her young married years, the concern for her brothers and sisters far away never left her thoughts.

She was a self-educated woman who had a cunning insight into life. Her no-nonsense approach could sometimes be a little surprising to her listener, but she always called a spade a spade. Her quiet courage and strength, and her inner and outer beauty, are only some of the reasons that we are proud to be her children.

Because of the tenor of the times when these events took place, and because the mores of the people of that period are so germaine to this story, I have included a relevant variety of historical vignettes. These historical snapshots help better to understand the mind set of the people of that period.

The reader will observe very shortly that the taxi industry played an integral part in my parents' early and middle lives. The cause and effect results of my father's loyalty to the Checker Taxi Company also were very apparent in the early trials and tribulations of this fledgling industry.

CHAPTER ONE

Philip and Bella Fox's life journey together was long, arduous and bountiful. It was filled, as most marital unions are, with sorrow, joy, travail, and eventual bliss. Love was the matrix that bonded this wonderful mosaic together.

Their beginnings were totally diverse. Though both of Jewish heritage, they came from different host countries in Europe, where Jews were considered, at best, second class citizens, or, more commonly, not citizens at all. Bella was from Romania, a classic Catholic country that regarded all marriages and births non-existent if they were not consecrated by a priest in the local Catholic church.

Philip was from a small section of Europe known as Galicia. Always in a constant state of flux from its warring predator neighbors, Galician Jews enjoyed their greatest freedom under the rule of the Emperor Franz Joseph of the Austro-Hungarian Empire. Jews held offices in the government and all children were mandated to attend school.

Their story begins with Philip's arrival in the United States during the week of April 22, 1912, just seven days following the sinking of the "unsinkable ship," the Titanic, on its maiden voyage. On the crossing with him were his grandfather, mother, four sisters, a brother and an uncle. After clearing the immigration processing center at Ellis Island, New York, the family left for Chicago where Philip's father waited.

On their arrival in Chicago, the Fox family settled in a rented flat in the Jewish immigrant section of the city. Children were sent to schools in the neighborhood, and the adults went about trying to scratch out a living for their dependents. Times were stern and lean. Survival was the immediate goal of all newcomers.

Going to school every day was an adventure for the Fox children. Due to the heavy influx of new arrivals, the schools became crowded and the children had to go farther distances, through strange neighborhoods in order to attend classes. The neighborhoods of greatest concern were the Italian and Polish sections of the immigrant settlements. The taunts and catcalls of the Italian and Polish children rang in the ears of the Fox kids twice a day, once going to school and once on their way home. "Kike," "Jew bastard," "greenhorn," and "sheenie," were the common epithets hurled.

The level of vitriolic abuse heaped upon one people by another depended on the amount of time you were in the "Promised Land." As you moved up the economic ladder, and your use of the English language improved, it was common practice to taunt the people on the socio-economic rung below you. The situation usually became intolerable and fights ensued. It was these conditions that either toughened you or forced you to become reticent and defensive in nature.

Phil Fox and his brother Jack became hardened combatants, taking on all comers from all ethnic groups surrounding the Jewish enclave. These pugnacious experiences during the tender years of eleven through seventeen formed them into men with a chip on their shoulders. As they entered the working world this chip always reminded them that they were as good as anyone, and they were ready to fight to prove it. The term "Rough Boys" was given to the Fox brothers early in their working careers, and stayed with them for years afterwards.

Automobiles were, in every aspect, the early love of Phil Fox. His fondness for cars started at a young age, and continued all the years of his life. It was his love affair with the auto that attracted him and his brother Jack to the taxi industry, and the purchase of their first taxi.

In 1917, John Hertz founded the Yellow Taxi Company. This was the same John Hertz who many years later created the internationally known Hertz Rent-a-Car Corporation. As the Yellow Taxi Company was growing and its ridership increased, other independent drivers began forming associations. Under the leadership of Frank Dilger, these associations became the Checker Taxi Company.

By 1918, Philip and Jack had purchased their first automobile, a 1918 Dodge touring car, and their taxi permit. They shared the duties of driving, each one of them taking a twelve hour shift; one driving days and the other driving at night. They were single, confident, and tough, and were sure they could overcome any obstacle that would stand in their way.

Two events of great consequence took place in this second decade of the Twentieth Century. World War I came to an end in 1918, and at about the same time, the Volstead Act (Prohibition) was coursing its way through the state legislatures, on the way to becoming the Eighteenth Amendment to the Constitution of the United States. These two occurrences were the impetus that launched the infamous 1920s. The "Roaring Twenties" and the "Unruly Decade" were just two of the names given to these ten years in American life, the likes of which were never seen before, and have never been seen since. It was during this period that Chicago gained the reputation as the gangster capital of the world which it has yet to live down. The mere mention of the name Chicago conjures up the image of gangsters, guns, and booze.

On January 16, 1920, at 12:01 a.m,. the United States began drying out. Prohibition was to last almost fourteen years, uncorking a decade of decadence, debilitation, drunkenness, debauchery, speakeasies, bootleggers, gangsters, mayhem and murder. Illegal booze begat fortunes for the smallest "bathtub gin" bottlers to the largest hidden warehouse distilleries. Money was no object in this decade of "Anything Goes."

For 350 years or so, our fledgling nation had existed under a fairly restrictive moral and religious code, thanks to its Puritan origins. While growing up, it had to endure wars and hardships, and all of the pangs that come with maturity. Then, by the year 1920, a crazy phenomenon occurred. The entire country unlaced its collective corset, metaphorically to "Let it all hang out." It took more than ten years once again to cinch up this moral girdle, and return the population to normality, idealism and its moral religious upbringing.

Competition in the transportation world became extremely fierce. In addition to the hauling and transporting of people and cargo, vehicles of every size and shape were employed to move illegal whiskey and beer to their thirsty destinations. Inventive minds created thousands of various containers to convey this illicit liquid. Free flowing alcohol and free flowing money gave rise to the likes of "Public Enemy Number One," crime czar Al Capone, while at the other end of the spectrum, locked in combat with the rising crime czar and his cohorts, was the incorruptible Untouchable, Elliott Ness, the nemesis of the underworld.

CHAPTER TWO

In his rush to adulthood and the completion of his Americanization, Philip took a bride on January 10, 1921, at the tender age of twenty. The girl he met and married was a young lady of nineteen named Dora Rubin. This marriage was doomed to failure from its very inception. Dora was an American-born girl. Her parents had climbed out of the immigrant repository of Chicago, and had become more socially and financially secure. Perhaps due to their youth, Philip and Dora's views on marriage differed greatly. Each of them refused to concede any point and were unwilling to reach a compromise to settle into a happy marriage. She felt that her husband should support her in the manner to which she was accustomed. Cooking and cleaning had been done for her and she expected this to continue. Dora's adamant refusal to conduct her wifely duties, as envisioned by Philip, to cook his meals and wash and mend his clothes, kept the unhappy atmosphere of their marriage from changing.

Philip was aggressive, industrious, and very fastidious in his habits and appearance. He expected his life to be ordered in a particular way. He wanted to have his own home before they raised a family. In this enlightened dawning of the twenties, single women and young married women without children were entering the work force in ever increasing numbers. Philip suggested to Dora that perhaps in lieu of performing her household chores, she should go to work and help to secure financially the American Dream. Dora absolutely refused, and that is where the impasse remained. Philip left their residence on March 15, 1921, and never returned. Dora filed for divorce on May 23, 1921, and the final decree was issued February 17, 1922. The actual time spent together as man and wife was just two and one-half months. It was time for Philip to get on with his life.

Taxicabs were the transportation of choice for the rich and famous high rollers. People gravitated to Chicago, renowned as the mecca for flappers, great jazz music, and the infamous gangsters. It was the capital of the Midwest. This new era in Chicago also saw the rise of the Thompson-Small-Lundin political machine. It was considered one of the most corrupt and crooked political organizations in American history. William Hale Thompson, known as "Big Bill," was mayor of Chicago during most of the raucous twenties, and Len Small was the Governor of the State of Illinois. John Lundin was a political operator who wound his way through City Hall and city politics. Phil and Jack Fox found themselves in the middle of this chaotic atmosphere.

In late 1920, John Hertz, president and founder of the Yellow Taxi Company, convinced his pal "Big Bill" to introduce a bill in the City Council, creating an ordinance known as the "Cab Stand Permit Law." In order for a taxicab driver in the city of Chicago to join in the line at hotels or other predetermined places to pick up fares, he had to pay a fee to the city of Chicago and display his permit. The hidden flaw in this bill was the tacit understanding by the people administering it that unless you were a Yellow Taxi driver working for Mr. Hertz, your application was never accepted. The war was on.

Fist fights, smashed windows, brick throwing, mayhem and even gun shots, were just some of the methods employed in the daily pursuit of earning a living during the early months of 1921. By this time, Phil and Jack had become dedicated and loyal drivers in the Checker Taxi organization. In the middle of this taxicab carnage was Phil Fox leading the charge to correct this injustice to Checker Taxi drivers and the other independent driver-owners who were separated from their daily fares by this corrupt and insidious law.

On the night of June 8, 1921, the world fell apart for Philip Fox. The battle began early in the evening at the cab stand in front of the Sherman Hotel in downtown Chicago. Drivers of the Yellow Cab Company and the Checker Cab Company were engaged in several altercations including fist fights, brick throwing, and smashing of each others' cabs. Sparked by the incident at the Sherman Hotel, other hostilities erupted in and around Chicagoland. One Yellow Cab driver was shot in the foot in Logan Square. A Checker Cab driver was surrounded by four Yellow cabs at 33rd Street and Michigan Avenue, and had his car rammed into the curb, smashing his wheels and windows. W. Winch, a Checker chauffeur, claimed that five Yellow Cab drivers attacked him, and all the windows in his cab were smashed. Nobody was safe during these melees, passengers, drivers, or pedestrians. Bedlam on the Chicago streets continued through the rest of the evening and on into the early hours of June 9th. The violence came to an end that morning with the murder of Thomas A. Skirven, a Yellow Cab driver.

Unknown to Philip, that same evening, his brother Jack was involved in another incident that could have had similar consequences. All Checker drivers who were working the evening of June 8 were alerted to the fracas at the Sherman Hotel and the resulting damage and injuries. They were told to be aware of any other incidents, and come to the aid of their fellow drivers. Jack had been driving the taxi he and Philip shared, pursuing his nightly routine, picking up fares and then returning to the various cab stands, awaiting new passengers. After dispensing one of his customers and returning to a downtown taxi stand, Jack's cab was fired upon by a rival Yellow cab moving up quickly from the rear.

Jack, who from early childhood was not easily intimidated, extracted his own .32 caliber revolver from under the seat, and started to return the fire. The gun battle became heated as both cabs came racing down Roosevelt Road, side by side, returning each other's gunfire. As they approached the intersection of Racine Avenue, a policeman who was standing on the corner observed the two speeding vehicles, and noticed the one driven by Jack had fired a shot. He immediately assumed that Jack was the aggressor in this running gun duel, and signaled the Yellow cab to stop. After observing the Checker turning north onto Racine Avenue, he then climbed onto the "running board" of the Yellow cab to pursue the speeding Checker. The officer began firing his weapon at the Checker cab in front of him. Jack, not looking back, began returning the gunfire, not realizing that it was a police officer doing the shooting. When Jack turned left onto Harrison Street, he first noticed the police officer standing on the side of the Yellow cab firing at him.

On Harrison Street just past the corner was a Checker Cab garage. The night manager was his best friend, Abe Schwartz. Jack took the corner on two wheels. He slammed on the brakes of his cab, abandoned the vehicle and darted into the open overhead door of the garage. The police officer leaped from the running board of the Yellow cab and went off in hot pursuit of Jack on foot. As the officer approached the door, Jack's friend Abe stepped in front of him, demanding to know where he was going. Abe informed the officer that he was on private property and without the proper search warrant he could not let him on the premises. The officer informed Abe that he was in pursuit of a suspected felon and that Abe was impeding his apprehension. Abe tried to stand firm on the grounds he just explained, but the officer was not interested in any more conversation. He proceeded to arrest Abe for the crime of obstruction of justice.

Jack, taking advantage of the delaying tactics of his friend, made for the rear exit, and was able to make it to safety. A short time later, Jack called to the garage hoping his friend Abe was able to convince the officer to drop the matter, as no one was injured in this fracas. Jack learned that Abe was arrested and taken to the Maxwell Street station for interrogation. Fearing the physical nature of the questioning might force Abe to reveal his identity, Jack figured the best course of action at this point in time, was to make himself as scarce as possible until the incident was forgotten. Not knowing about the trouble his brother Philip was about to encounter, Jack left for South Bend, Indiana, and the sanctuary offered by relatives.

The .32 caliber revolver that Jack had been firing was to become an important part of the evidence used against Philip in the oncoming days. Because they shared a locker in the garage in which their cab was housed, it was easy for any of the drivers to see the gun that belonged to Jack and assume that it was Philip's.

CHAPTER THREE

The morning headlines screamed the story "Driver Slain in Taxi War; $5,000 Reward." The article below the headlines told the story of the fatal attack. "Skirven was standing in front of the Yellow Cab stand at Roosevelt Road and Kedzie Avenue talking to fellow chauffeurs. A large automobile, said by several witnesses to have been a Stutz, sped north on Kedzie Avenue."

"Three of the occupants of the auto opened fire with revolvers. Over twenty-five shots were fired at the men standing on the sidewalk, one bullet struck Skirven in the left side above the heart. He was rushed to St. Anthony's Hospital where he was pronounced dead. The Yellow Cab Company at 2:00 a.m. this morning offered a reward of $5,000.00 for the arrest and conviction of the slayers of Skirven."

Accusations and recriminations began to fill the newspapers. Leaders of both cab companies accused each other of initiating the taxi wars. "'We have gone just as far as we are going to go with the murderous methods of the Checker Taxi Company,' said John Hertz, president of the Yellow Cab Company." The retaliatory charge came swiftly from Checker Taxi president Mike Sokol. At a hearing before the committee on local transportation, trying to end the war between the cab companies, president Sokol charged "that the police and city officials helped the Yellow Cab company since the taxi wars started. Checker has been fighting the entire Thompson-Lundin political organization."

The two contradictory versions of the arrest of Philip were indicative of the convoluted and biased direction this case was about to take. According to the early edition of the *Chicago Tribune*, June 10, 1921, "Philip Fox was arrested early yesterday morning in the restaurant and pool room of David J. Brown, 2002 W. Division St." This arrest was supposed to have taken place around 1:00 a.m. on the morning of June 9, 1921.

In an obvious contradiction of the newspaper account ten months later in sworn testimony in the first trial, Police Detective Thomas J. Mangan stated under oath that he "arrested Fox at his home about 9:00 o'clock that morning; and that when he started down

CHECKER CAB DRIVER NAMES 5 IN SLAYING

Company Heads Lay Blame on Politics.

Philip Fox, 2342 Washburne avenue, Checker Cab company chauffeur, confessed last night that he was implicated in the murder of Thomas A. Skirven, driver of a Yellow cab.

He named five companions who were with him in the big car from which the shots were fired. They had been touring the city all night, he said, doing 'al the damage they could to Yellow cabs.

T. A. SKIRVEN.

New Action in Bitter War.

This was the latest development in the bitter war that has been raging between the rival cab companies for some time. Others are—

Two men in a Yellow cab fired four shots at Joseph Zomowski, 5109 Melvina avenue, a Checker chauffeur, at California and Grand avenue last night. None of the shots took effect.

Harry Rosenthal, n, Checker driver, reported that he was sitting in his cab at 22d and Halsted streets late last night and was fired upon by the occupants of a large touring car tha, sped past south on Halsted street. The driver was ...

Chicago Tribune, June 10, 1921

the Yellow Cab company and independents.

Charge Politics Back of War.

Officials of the Checker company also declare that politics and unionism are back of the war, that they are "fighting the entire Thompson-Lundin political organization."

Fox was arrested early yesterday morning in the restaurant and pool room of David J. Brown, 2002 West Division street. He admitted he and the other Checker employes went there to hide their revolvers after the shooting of Skirven.

His confession came after the Yellow Cab company had offered a reward of $5,000 for the arrest of Skirven's

resolution calling on Chief of Police Fitzmorris to keep both the Yellow and the Checker cabs off the streets until such time as they can guarantee to quit fighting. This is designed to protect the lives of taxicab passengers, which, in the present state of affairs, the aldermen say, are unsafe. This can be done, they point out, by revoking their licenses.

"Fifty Checker chauffeurs were arrested in the loop, practically every Checker chauffeur who ventured into the First precinct was taken into custody on the charge that he had no cab stand license.

Officials of the Checker cab company say they tendered a check for $3,750 to the vehicle bureau last December to obtain cab and licenses. S. Stupner, secretary, declares the check was returned though licenses were issued to

avenue last night. None of the shots took effect.

Harry Rosenthal, a Checker driver, reported that he was sitting in his cab at 22d and Halsted streets late last night and was fired upon by the occupants of a large touring car that sped past south on Halsted street. The driver was unharmed, but the car was riddled with bullets.

The same car is said to have fired upon two police officers standing at 35th street and Kedzie avenue a short time later. The police returned the fire but reported no one was injured.

Aldermen to Take Action.

Aldermen George M. Maypole and Joseph O. Kostner will introduce in the city council meeting today a

6 CHECKER TAXI MEN INDICTED IN DRIVERS' WAR

Grand Jury Acts Quickly In Murder of T. A. Skirven of Yellow Cab.

Five employes of the Checker Taxi company were indicted today for the murder of T. A. Skirven, a driver for the Yellow Cab company, who was shot and killed early yesterday, after rival chauffeurs had waged a guerrilla war thru the streets for two nights.

A sixth Checker man was indicted for conspiracy to murder and assault to kill. All the indictments were based on confessions said to have been made by two of the six men. Philip Fox of 2242

Washburn avenue, one of the Checker drivers who, the police say, admitted that he took part in the attack on Skirven, repudiated his confession after the murder indictment had been voted against him by the grand jury.

Fox Charges Slugging.

Appearing before Judge Francis S. Wilson, Fox asserted that he had been slugged by three police officers in the state attorney's office and compelled to make false statements.

Attorney Leonard Grossman, representing the company, accused the state's attorney and the city administration of persecuting the Checker drivers because of politics.

He said he would go before Attorney General Edward J. Brundage and ask for an impartial investigation of the entire matter.

It is admitted by Mr. Stewart, the assistant state's attorney, that Judge George F. Barrett, former law partner of State's Attorney Crowe, was with him when Fox all night, questioning him, said Grossman. "Judge Barrett is chief counsel for the Yellow Cab company. I do not believe that is fair treatment."

Fox's charges were called "absurd" by the prosecutors.

The other men indicted are:
MORRIS STEUBEN, 1803 South Millard avenue, said to have confessed.

that the manager allowed a chauffeur, who was being sought by the policeman, and who was hiding in the garage, to escape.

According to the policeman, he was at Racine avenue and Roosevelt road when he saw a Yellow cab and a Checker cab racing toward him, went in Roosevelt road. At the intersection, he said, the Checker cab turned north in Racine avenue and the chauffeur fired two shots at the Yellow cab chauffeur. The policeman boarded the Yellow cab and gave chase. He fired several shots at the Checker driver, which were returned by the chauffeur. The exchange of shots continued until the driver reached the company's garage on Harrison street, where he ran in and hid.

Pawelzyk followed and demanded that Schwartz turn the driver over to him, and while they were talking, he said, the chauffeur escaped.

Chauffeur Makes Getaway.

Schwartz was taken to the Maxwell street station, and he will be questioned in an effort to make him turn the chauffeur over to the police. Several more fights between chauffeurs

(Continued on Next Page.)

JOSEPH DVORJKA, address unknown, said to have confessed that he was with the others just before the murder. Charged with conspiracy.

JAMES MOTLEY, address unknown. Murder.

CHARLES GOLDSTEIN, address unknown. Murder.

MAX PODOSKI, address unknown. Murder.

Three Are Fugitives.

Motley, Goldstein and Podoski have not yet been arrested, the detectives have been searching for them ever since the confessions were made.

The indictments were obtained by William Scott Stewart, who went before the grand jury immediately after receiving the police report on the confessions.

While he was laying his evidence before the grand jury, other city and county officials were taking drastic action to end the taxicab war, which has been going on sporadically for months.

Manager Is Arrested.

Abraham Schwartz, night manager of a Checker Cab garage at 1124 Harrison street, was arrested early today by Policeman Stanley Pawelzyk on a charge

CONFESSION IN TAXI WAR IS REPUDIATED

Charging that he was taken into a back room of the state's attorney's office and slugged and beaten, Philip Fox, employe of the Checker Taxicab Company, today before Judge Francis S. Wilson made a complete repudiation of his confession in the shooting and killing of P. A. Skirven, a driver for the Yellow Cab Company.

The grand jury had just voted true bills, it was reported, charging Fox and five other alleged employes of the Checker company with murder, conspiracy and assault to kill. Fox, Morris Steuben, 1503 S. Millard av.; James Morley, Charles Goldstein and Max Podwski were said to have been named in the Skirven murder.

Fox and Steuben and a third man, name withheld, had confessed, it was said, that they were in a touring car from which the fatal shots were fired. Joseph Devolka, also alleged to be a Checker employe, was reported named in a true bill on a charge of conspiracy and assault to kill John Lawrence, a Yellow cab chauffeur, who was shot in the foot.

The city council today adopted a resolution introduced by Alderman George F. Maypole which demands that the taxicab warfare cease forthwith and instructs Chief of Police Charles C. Fitzmorris to revoke the licenses of all chauffeurs employed by the rival companies unless the campaign of shooting and slugging ends. As originally introduced the measure provided that the chief re-

Continued on Page 2, Column 8.

CONFESSION IN TAXI DEATH IS REPUDIATED

Continued From First Page.

voke the licenses at 1 p. m. Monday unless conditions grew better. This was later amended, however, to give Chief Fitzmorris discretionary power.

CHIEF IS AROUSED.

Meanwhile Chief of Police Fitzmorris announced that unless the taxi war ceased he would issue a special order directing that police search all drivers and occupants of both Yellow and Checker cabs and if revolvers are found prosecute them under the drastic Sadler act. He said the police were

wholly impartial, that they will be as severe against one company as the other.

Fox repudiated his confession while his counsel, Attorney Joseph Harrington, was seeking a writ of habeas corpus for his release. Attorney Leonard Grossman for the Checker company charged that "everybody's against the Checker people." He said he would ask Attorney General Edward Brundage for a full inquiry.

SAYS CONFESSION FORCED.

"It was admitted here, Judge Wilson, that ex-Judge George F. Barrett, former law partner of State's Attorney Crowe and now chief counsel for the Yellow Cab Company, has been with Fox in the state's attorney's office all night. I do not believe that is fair.

"We can't get a square deal from Crowe or the police. Fox repudiates his confession in the Skirven murder. He was slugged and beaten in a back room of Crowe's office. They made him confess."

"Look at my lips," said Fox, displaying cuts. "Look at my shirt, ...

the street with him, Fox asked, 'What is this for? Is this about that shooting over on Twelfth Street?' I then asked him what he knew about the shooting and Fox answered that he had read about it in the paper."

However the arrest occurred, Philip was brought to the offices of the Cook County State's Attorney, Robert E. Crowe. He was arrested without a warrant, and was held incommunicado in the State's Attorney's office for the next several days. He was brought in and out of a dark room where for hours at a time he was beaten, kicked, vilified, and threatened with further violence if he did not confess. Morris Stuben, who had been arrested at about the same time as Fox, was subjected to the same treatment.

Morris Stuben and Philip and Jack Fox had been friends since the Fox family arrived from Europe and had settled in their first neighborhood. Morris was a couple of years older than Philip, but they became fast friends right at the outset. The three of them played and socialized all through their teenage years. They started their careers together as cab drivers. Through all the years of their trials and incarceration, and the rest of their lives, they remained solid friends.

Attorney George F. Barrett and his associate Benjamin Samuels, who conducted the interrogations were neither members of the State's Attorney's staff nor officials of the police department. Both men were attorneys for the Yellow Cab Company, and Barrett was a former law partner of State's Attorney Crowe. One police officer, whom Philip did not know, asked him if he knew Barrett, who was then just passing while they were in the corridor sitting on a bench. When Fox said he did not know him, and had never seen him before, the officer stated to him that it was "Judge" Barrett, and that he was the person in charge of the investigation, and that Fox better come clean and tell them what they wanted to know. Philip was not aware of the fact that Attorney Barrett was an ex-judge who had resigned from the bench eight months earlier, and had no official capacity in that office.

Between deprivation of sleep, beatings, and long periods of time spent in the dark room, Philip was at the point of confessing to anything in order to stop the unbearable treatment. The last act of terror in the dark room prior to the confession came when the two police officers, named Davern and Bernacchi, became extremely aggressive. Bernacchi bent down with his knees in Philip's stomach and said to him, "Come clean, you little son-of-a-bitch, or I'll throw you out of the window." Bernacchi continued to knee him for at least five more minutes, while officer Davern kicked him in the shins, and beat him about the head. He was again taken before Barrett, who began to interrogate him by asking, "Do you know anything about it now?" Philip answered that he did not, but would say anything that he (Barrett) wanted to hear in order to end the torture. He then signed his confession at 3:00 a.m.

Later that morning Fox and Stuben were taken before the Grand Jury. They appeared without the benefit of counsel, and only in the presence of the jury members and people from the State's Attorney's office. However, there is an indication that there was one other person present, who was allowed to sit in with no official sanction to justify his presence. This person was Mr. Benjamin Samuels, counsel for the Yellow Cab Company. Following the Grand Jury hearings, several True Bills of indictments were handed down. They read as follows:

G.J. No. 147
   The People of the State of Illinois vs. Philip Fox et al.
   Indictment for Assault with intent to Murder
                                        Bail - $10,000.00 each

G.J. No. 148
   The People of the State of Illinois vs. Philip Fox et al.
   Indictment for Murder
                                        Bail - No Bail

G.J. No. 149
   The People of the State of Illinois vs. Philip Fox et al.
   Indictment for Conspiracy to commit Murder
                                        Bail - $10,000.00 each

The "et al." in all three indictments were Morris Stuben, John Doveika, James Mogley, Charles Goldstein, and Max Podolsky. Later, during several bail bond hearings, the bond amounts were reduced and John Doveika was removed from two of the three indictments.

As we will see later on during the pardon hearing, the other three men allegedly in the same car as Fox and Stuben were never really identified as to affiliation. James Mogley, Charles Goldstein and Max Podolsky, although indicted, were never tried due to lack of evidence. If they were not employees of the cab company or the drivers union, where did they come from, and what were they doing in the fingered automobile?

It is a known fact that the Torrio-Capone mob had been employed all through the political years of the Thompson administration. It is also a known fact that Thompson and John Hertz were allies. So it is easy to put together the theory that the Torrio-Capone mob was also employed by John Hertz and the Yellow Cab Company during the taxicab wars. Following this line of reasoning, the opposing muscle for the Checker Cab Company must have been members of the Jewish Gangs, possibly the Davey Miller boys. This probably is how Mogley, Goldstein, and Podolsky were connected by the police to the investigation.

In the habeas corpus hearing, held the next morning in the courtroom of Judge Francis Wilson, Philip emphatically denied the confession he had made under duress and the "third degree" methods employed by the people in the State's Attorney's office. Philip charged that he was beaten, abused and threatened with the loss of his life if he did not confess. In addition to the physical trauma, Philip also displayed extreme emotional distress, when he declared outright to Judge Wilson, "Look at my lips," displaying cuts. "Look at my shirt, they tore off all my buttons. Look at my hair. They kept slugging and beating me, I cried for mercy. They would not let me sleep." True to his fastidious nature, he was troubled by the fact that he was forced to appear in public in this disheveled condition. Elvert M. Allen, a court reporter, corroborated Philip's story as to his mussed-up condition, and volunteered his own personal comb to Philip to try to restore some semblance of neatness to his appearance.

Morris Stuben concurred as to the same treatment given to him. Judge Wilson, upon hearing all the testimony, ruled in favor of

Fox and Stuben, and ordered them to be removed from the custody of the State's Attorney and to be turned over to the Sheriff's Department. He then continued the writ hearing until the following Tuesday. While Philip was in the custody of the Sheriff's Department, he was examined by three doctors: Dr. Omens, a prominent dermatologist; Dr. Martusson, chief of medicine at Jackson Park Hospital; and the jail doctor. Upon completion of the examinations, Philip was transferred to the prison hospital, where he spent a considerable amount of time recuperating from his injuries.

The report of the three doctors' examination read as follows: "Fox was found to be in a highly nervous condition, and appeared like a man who had been terrorized. He was found to have a hematoma, or blood clot, on the top of his head, with a raised swelling about half as high as a large egg; an abrasion behind the left ear, and another on the skull, on the same side; bruises on the neck below the left ear and bruises on the right shoulder; a swelling and bruises on the left arm; and bruises, abrasions, or little cuts in the skin and anterior aspect of the tibia or shin bone. There were also abrasions and cuts on the mucous membranes on the inside of his mouth and cuts on the upper lip. The bruises were discernible, and you could easily see one side was bruised, though not much swollen, yet cut a good deal more than the other side. There was some swelling on the jaw and some discoloration.

"Stuben, generally speaking, was in better condition than Fox, and did not have the extreme nervousness that Fox displayed. He had bruises on the anterior aspect on both shin bones, and the same kind [*sic*] of marks that Fox had, with cuts and bruises on both shin bones and deep bruises and swelling, over the right deltoid muscles that round out the shoulders; and on the right side of the chest, at the edge of the ribs, he found a long discoloration or deep bruise. He also had a loose tooth--upper incisor. Dr. Omens corroborated Dr. Martusson in these examinations, but states that he was pretty sure that Stuben's tooth was knocked out or extremely loose, and that his lip was lacerated under the tooth, on the inside. These examinations took place on June 10th and they also examined the defendants on the 11th. Conclusion: the wounds were recently made."

CHAPTER FOUR

After the arrest, the Grand Jury indictments and the habeas corpus hearings, the matter of raising money for the bail fell upon Philip's family. Max Fox, Philip's dad, whose life had been dedicated to providing for his family, never hesitated in putting up the family home for security for the bail money. In spite of the initial shame of the arrest, the family stood by him as a solid unit, ready to sacrifice and provide whatever was necessary to prove the innocence of their beloved son and brother.

True to the prediction of John Hertz, the cab wars did subside with the arrest of Philip Fox and Morris Stuben (who had been identified by witnesses as the driver of the car). The cab companies now had their "sacrificial lambs." They were the balm to soothe the fires of the beleaguered industry. Greed and the power machinations of the owners, along with the illegal activities of the drivers, continued unabated, but the fear of Federal intervention subsided with the arrests in the Skirven murder. The Thompson-Small-Lundin political organization was still flying high. John Hertz and his Yellow Cab Company were political allies. Opposing the organization were the Reform coalition candidates, supported by the Checker Taxi Company and independent drivers.

It became very apparent that whom you supported in Chicago politics determined how you got treated by the police, State's Attorney's office and City Hall. Following a dinner and political fund raiser for the opposing Coalition Candidates, arrests and harassment by the police of the Checker drivers hit an all time high. Malicious abuse of the legal process was used openly to intimidate those who opposed the machine. Charges and counter-charges continued to fill the Chicago dailies.

Politics in the twenties was no different than politics today. It may not have been as well honed or as polished as it is now, but it was politics nonetheless. Every incoming immigrant group soon learned that in the United States, politics was the avenue to power. It was the vehicle that could secure them a position in the mainstream of American life, and guarantee them considerable economic muscle.

But it was not as simple as it sounded. It required tremendous effort on the part of the organizers to educate and convince the new populace of the necessity to become citizens and gain the right to vote. Without the vote they had no foundation. That was the genesis of all political power. From this first building block, they then moved to the various factions already organized and operating.

Labor was the prize on which they set their sights. The Jewish people brought their established work guilds and associations with them when they came from Europe. It required the necessary marriage of politics and labor to give impetus to their political organization. The labor movement itself was in another evolutionary funk with the introduction of the technology of mass production. Old jobs were being eliminated faster than new jobs were being created. It was a must for Labor to affiliate itself with the politicians in order to gain "clout" in Chicago. Clout meant contracts and more jobs.

However strong the new political groups grew, they were never quite powerful enough to dislodge the incumbents. Thus this impasse brought about the nefarious strong-arm tactics employed by all sides in this bloody grab for power in Chicago.

It was obvious from the beginning that the Taxi Wars were in themselves due to the volatile political situation in Chicago. Any attempt to build an opposition to the Thompson Administration was met by swift retaliation. Because they had the audacity to back the Reform candidates, the Checker Association was targeted for harassment. One method employed was the enactment of the infamous "Cab Stand Permit" law. Agents of the Thompson administration infiltrated opposition rallies and carefully noted which drivers were in attendance. The next day these same drivers were pulled over, ticketed and often hassled by the Chicago Police. John Hertz was a valued backer of the Thompson regime, and his wishes were usually carried out against his competitors.

In the habeas corpus hearing before Judge Wilson concerning the shooting death of Yellow Cab driver T.A. Skirven, attorney Leonard Grossman, representing Philip Fox, Morris Stuben, and Checker Taxi, accused "the State's Attorney and the city administration of persecuting the Checker drivers because of politics."

He said he would go before the Attorney General of Illinois and ask for a complete and impartial investigation of the entire political situation in Chicago. As far as history shows, no investigation ever took place. Dirty, crooked politics continued unabated until the temporary interruption with the election of reform-minded Democratic mayor William E. Dever in 1923.

The new mayor's single-minded reform was to try to enforce the now dreaded prohibition law hated by the very thirsty electorate of the City of Chicago. The effort by the mayor fell far short of its goal, and paved the way for the return of the disreputable Thompson machine. This was the time when the Jewish-led West Side Democratic organization began to flex its muscles.

Small Jewish gangs which had been around since before the turn of the century had now been given stimulus for growth and strength. It was these Jewish toughs who offered their services to protect the local Jewish merchants from harassment and burglaries by other ethnic gangs. They also provided the force to protect political rallies from disruption and physical mayhem attempted by hirelings from clashing political parties.

Davey Miller's restaurant, pool hall, gym and gambling emporium was the gathering point for these Jewish protectors. It was from this central location at 3216 Roosevelt Road that they, under the leadership of Davey Miller and his brothers, fanned throughout the city protecting the religious teachers, students and merchants from unrelenting harassment. Davey Miller in his own way was a true folk hero of the Jewish West Side. Just eight doors down at the corner on the Kedzie Avenue side was the Yellow Cab stand where Yellow Cab driver Thomas Skirven was shot and fatally wounded.

Next door to Davey Miller's was the headquarters for the burgeoning 24th Ward Democratic Organization. Philip and his brother Jack were very eager participants in the activities of the Democratic Party during this period. They attended political rallies, and money raising functions to bolster the strength of the organization. The Democrats of Chicago felt the opportunity was approaching to unseat the corrupt Thompson machine. It would require the combined power of all the diverse neighborhoods to topple this unethical Republican administration.

Sometime during the middle 1920s the aspirations of the Democratic Party of Chicago came to fruition due to the political wizardry of Anton Cermak. He forged the vital links between each of the uniquely different neighborhoods and cemented the coalition until his tragic death on March 6, 1933. The powerful organization he put together remained intact from his demise to the very end of Chicago's other powerhouse mayor, Richard J. Daley, who died in 1976.

CHAPTER FIVE

During the year between the indictment and trial, Philip had reached his maturity, and was able to vote in his first election. It was at this point in time that he made a career change, and became an apprentice plumber. Still single, he worked very hard, long hours in a trade that required a great amount of physical strength. Helping to support his family was his primary concern, but he also took the opportunity to educate himself further, and continued to champion the causes of individual rights and liberties.

Philip's concerns for the upcoming trial were placated by the officers and attorneys of the Checker Taxi Company. Mike Sokol, president of the company, constantly reminded Philip that everything was taken care of and that he had nothing to worry about. He assured them they had the finest lawyers available in Chicago. With no eyewitnesses, the State had a very weak case at best. He was told that all the drivers and garage and maintenance men were behind him and Morris Stuben 100 percent. The drivers realized that what Philip and Morris had set out to do the night of June 8th was to try to right a wrong that had been done to them and the other 1,500 Checker drivers and independents. In his youth and zeal, Philip did not realize that their method of redress had been misguided, and that it would have such disastrous consequences.

As the April 1922 term of the Criminal Court of Cook County approached, Philip's attorneys, paid by the Checker Taxi Company, prepared their defense. They were not aware at this time that this would be the first in a series of hearings, delays and continuances that would last for four more years. The confidence level of the defendants and the Checker Taxi attorneys remained high throughout the first trial.

The Honorable George Kersten presided. Former Judge William Heath led the charge for the Prosecution. The State asked for the death penalty, and began to qualify the jury as to their belief in the death penalty by hanging. Having found twelve persons who so believed, the trial proceeded. Mr. Heath, in his opening statement before the jury, demanded that the two defendants be sentenced to death.

In ruling on the admissibility of the alleged confessions of Fox and Stuben, Judge Kersten issued this opinion: "[I]nasmuch as one of the confessions was received by a man to whom the confessor thought to be an officer of the court (i.e., Judge Barrett), it was not proper to be admitted; that the other confession was obtained by violence and fear and by third degree methods, it is also therefore not admissible in evidence."

Testifying for the prosecution at this first trial were two key witnesses, David J. Brown, proprietor of Brown's Restaurant and Pool Room, and Peter Hanson, a mysterious figure in the investigation of this case. David J. Brown testified "that three of the four men came into the restaurant shortly after 3:00 a.m., June 9th, and walked through the door that leads to the pool room; that there is a toilet in that room which is often used by the public; that the pool room is used as a Checker Taxi station until 1:00 a.m., when it is closed, and that after that time the restaurant is headquarters for Checker Taxi chauffeurs: that the men were in the pool room three or four minutes, and then went out; that he did not recognize any one of the men, except defendant Fox; that he saw Hanson around the restaurant several different times that night."

Peter Hanson testified "that shortly after 3:00 a.m. of the same morning he noticed a dark touring car stop in front of Brown's Restaurant, at 2003 W. Division Street; that five men stepped out of the car and walked into the restaurant and through a side door into a pool hall adjoining: that among these men were defendants Fox and Stuben; that they remained in the pool room a few minutes and then returned to the automobile and drove away. He testified further that the conduct of the five men aroused his suspicion and after they had gone, he went into the toilet in the pool hall to see if he could find anything there; that he found nothing, but later he made a further investigation, and found three guns under a porch at the rear of the pool hall." These guns he later delivered to Superintendent Katz of the Yellow Cab Company.

-33-

A number of questions regarding the testimony of Peter Hanson go begging for answers even to this day:

1. Who was Peter Hanson and for whom was he working?

2. What was he doing driving around Division Street at three o'clock in the morning?

3. Why had he been wandering in and out of Brown's Restaurant several times that evening, as testified to by the owner Brown?

4. Why would the so-called suspicious conduct by the five men compel him to go to the toilet in the pool hall to investigate? It is hard to conceive that anyone who was a passerby witness would go into a dark alley at three o'clock in the morning to conduct an investigation into an unknown crime.

5. The strangest question of all remains why Peter Hanson, upon the discovery of the weapons, did not go to the police and did not go to the State's Attorney, but instead delivered them to Superintendent Katz of the Yellow Cab Company?

Whether it was arrogance or ignorance, or some other more devious reason on the part of Defense Attorneys Joseph Harrington and Leonard J. Grossman to lay out the game plan for the defense as they did, we will never know. Whatever the reason, Fox and Stuben were never put on the stand to contradict the allegations brought before the jury by the prosecution witnesses. The reason the lawyers gave Philip and Morris for their confidence in the case, and not allowing the two defendants to be put on the witness stand, was a firm conviction that without the confessions, plus any trial errors that would arise, the Illinois Supreme Court would overturn any unfavorable ruling by the jury. Following the appearance of the two witnesses, Brown and Hanson, the police officers who made the initial arrests took the stand, and stated the various details of the apprehension of Fox and Stuben. The defense called no witnesses and then rested.

Judge Kersten charged the jury, and they went off to deliberate the verdict. After approximately twenty-four hours of deliberation, the jury informed the court that they were hopelessly deadlocked. Judge Kersten then dismissed the jury and declared a mistrial. It was later revealed that the jury had been hung at eleven to one in favor of a guilty verdict.

Influence being what it was back in 1922, the presumption is that it played a large part in State's Attorney Crowe's decision to go ahead with a new trial. It appeared his former law partner George Barrett, still chief legal counsel for the Yellow Cab Company, did not have to exert too much pressure on Crowe to proceed to a second trial. John Hertz continued to be adamant about his hatred of the other cab companies and their drivers, especially the Checker Taxi personnel, whom he considered riffraff, the low life of the industry. The sword of shame and danger had still not been lifted from above the head of Philip Fox.

CHAPTER SIX

The second half of 1921 and the first half of 1922 saw the local news headlines give way to national and international sensationalism. Governor Len Small of Illinois was himself on trial for fraud in Waukegan, Illinois. The Governor was accused of misappropriating $1.4 million in state funds while he was State Treasurer. At the conclusion of the trial, which lasted several weeks, Governor Small was finally acquitted.

Europe and other parts of the world seemed to be coming apart at the seams. President Wilson's League of Nations dream, although enthusiastically accepted by other nations, never could get adopted in the United States, due to the isolationist Congress and its leader, Henry Cabot Lodge. After a very sick and embittered President Wilson left office, the League of Nations just limped along as a world organization with very little power in world affairs. By 1922, the enforcement of the Treaty of Versailles, by virtue of its terms, allowed the Allies totally to eviscerate the economy of the defeated Germany, thus setting the stage for the rise of radicalism, Nazism, and Adolf Hitler, one short decade later.

The futility of the whole business of Prohibition was becoming more and more apparent. The entire nation had become obsessed with alcoholic beverages. Contempt for law and order had spread over the land. Graft and corruption were everywhere. The Prohibition law itself was full of loop holes, easily stepped through by the bootleggers and their high priced lawyers. Easy money was the vacuum used to suck every segment of the American population down into this national sinkhole of lawlessness.

Taxicab drivers became major players in this boozy and corrupt period of the early twenties. They carried the liquid contraband, as well as the patrons to the speakeasies and gin mills that flourished in Chicago. Drivers were given a fee for the "suckers"they delivered as well as for hauling the "goods." Bordellos and free-lance prostitutes alike kicked back to taxi drivers for the delivery of customers.

Death sentences and executions were the punishment of favor during the 1920s United States Attorney General A. Mitchell Palmer was the guru of the ultimate punishment. On a June evening in 1919, a powerful blast rocked his house. The discovery, on his front porch, of the burnt corpse of his would-be assassin surrounded by anarchist literature was all the incentive he needed to go forward on his mission to rid the United States of its radical "foreign" element.

Mass hysteria gripped the country, as hundreds of arrests occurred. The guilty and innocent alike were rounded up together. Deportation was the punishment used in milder cases, and stiff jail sentences and executions were used on the more violent ones. The example set forth by Mr. Palmer carried the length and breadth of the country. Local prosecuting attorneys followed his lead with slipshod trials and excessive punishment. Reactionary groups of all persuasions jumped on the bandwagon denouncing, degrading, persecuting and even killing people whom they felt were un-American and vastly different from themselves. The Ku Klux Klan was the most extreme of these groups. Their illegal and vigilante activities against immigrants, Blacks, Catholics, Jews and other groups not of their liking, have been burned into the memory and consciousness of this nation since the Civil War.

Corruption had not abated one iota in early 1923, having climbed straight to the White House and the administration of President Warren G. Harding. Charles R. Forbes, who was the Director of the Veterans Bureau and an Ohio crony of President Harding, was selling government medical supplies on the open market and receiving kickbacks on Veteran hospital contracts. Crime and immorality surrounded the Harding administration, and the infamous "Tea Pot Dome" scandal was its backbreaker. The perpetrators chose suicide by revolver rather than prison. Harding himself became extremely distressed by the double dealings of his appointees and on August 2, 1923, suffered a cerebral hemorrhage and died.

Strong unionism, fighting for better working conditions, became indistinguishable from the Anarchists, Socialists, Communists and radical movements in the eyes of the law enforcement community. This hysteria triggered mass arrests. Ten thousand people thought to be leftists were rounded up and arrested in 1920 alone. Palmer's excessive methods were criticized greatly by the more fair-minded citizens. His reply to them was that "this Red conspiracy must be stopped at all costs." An untold number of innocent immigrants were arrested, convicted and served time in jail. They believed they had joined the union for its collective protection and its goal of fair wages and equality in the workplace. Unions and radical groups were painted with the same brush by the Justice Department, headed by Palmer. In fairness to the Justice Department, however, several leaders of the trade unions had used the union pulpits to espouse their radical causes.

This boiling cauldron of extremism, fueled by management, labor, radicals, excessive force and police brutality went right on bubbling into the early and middle 1920s. As his first trial came to a close, Philip was swept up in this maelstrom, further heightening his awareness of the deplorable conditions of the working class world in these United States.

Waiting for the second trial to commence was an extreme ordeal for Philip, but everyday living forced this situation to a secondary position in his mind. He had progressed from an apprentice to a full scale journeyman in the plumbing trade. The plumbing union and its activities were beginning to occupy more of his time and thoughts. Workers were still looked down upon, and their rights were continually trampled on by management, court decisions and laws emanating from the halls of Congress. Labor strikes and picketing of workplaces had begun to decline from their zenith of over 3,000 strikes in 1919, but violence at job sites continued unabated.

CHAPTER SEVEN

Necessity of space and a slight rise in the economic status of the Fox family enabled them to purchase a four-flat building on the West Side of Chicago. It was an established path of movement created by previous Jewish immigrant families on their upwardly mobile climb. Philip's natural mechanical ability stood him well in the maintenance of the family home, and the contribution of a fair share of his income was needed in the Fox family's new lifestyle.

The family building, or mini-compound, although becoming a little more congested, remained a very viable and exciting place to live. Philip's two older sisters, Pauline and Fanny, had married a few years previously, and their families were growing larger with each new arrival. Mores and customs precluded children from leaving the family home until they were married. Unfortunately, the economics of the times brought the married children back home to the family safety net.

Religion and tradition played an extremely important part in the family life. A perfect example of the restrictions placed on single women by Jewish custom was illustrated in the teen years of Max and Marion's second child, Fanny. She was a lovely and happy child who filled her spare hours, between and after chores, with English and Yiddish songs, and dreams of performing on the Yiddish stage. Her ambition to display her talents came at an early age and grew stronger each day.

Somewhere around the age of sixteen years her desire to act and sing reached a feverish height. She summoned up all her young and determined courage, and asked her father's permission to participate in the upcoming auditions at the local Yiddish theater. Her trepidation was soon relieved as the broadening smile on her father's face got larger with each approaching step. He greeted her with the same warm affectionate embrace he always exhibited to all of his children.

After listening to Fanny's request, Max took a long time before he framed his answer. He thought of all the prohibitive traditions of his faith, and the possible damaging consequences to his daughter's reputation in the neighborhood. He wondered what long-lasting effect a disastrous audition would have on his young daughter's psyche. But on the other hand, how could he possibly disappoint this eager young face that was awaiting his reply?

Max gave his assent, and was immediately rewarded with a huge hug and kiss. She skipped out of the room with hope in her heart, and dreams of a bright future in the Yiddish entertainment world. It was later that evening that Max related to Marion their young daughter's request. He told Marion of his apprehensions, but also acknowledged Fanny's reaction to his approval.

Scarcely had Max finished before Marion angrily began itemizing the negatives in the now approved life choice of her daughter. The clucking of her tongue and the wagging of her finger punctuated the barrage of reasons of why she was so opposed. Max listened intently and found himself in agreement with a lot of the arguments his wife was making. He never realized the firestorm of protest his decision would unleash.

Taking into consideration all of the ramifications of a reversal of his decision, Max knew he was left with no choice. The next day, he called his aspiring entertainer into the living room. Looking into her sweet face, he tried to repeat all of the reasons and protestations laid out before him by her mother. The teenager listened as well as she possibly could, all the while realizing her father had changed his mind and was saying no ever so gently. Fanny was devastated. The later years of her life bore out the negative effects of this teenage trauma.

Jewish holidays and dietary laws were ardently observed by the family, under the watchful eye of the matriarch, Marion. She was the day to day ruler of this family, with her stiff backbone and magnificent pride. Little formal education did not prevent her from forging ahead in her Jewish world. Her business sense and fighting spirit came naturally. These attributes she passed down to her children and the progeny that followed.

Patriarch Max's role was of a different nature than his wife's. In his own style, he was the final arbiter in any altercation or family dispute. His quiet and loving manner, dovetailed with his keen sense of fair-mindedness, to bring about a satisfactory and just solution. He remained this highly principled and religious man throughout his entire life. The mantle of a "Tzadik" (a righteous person), was figuratively placed around his shoulders by his peers and all who knew him.

1922 passed into history, and 1923 saw very little change in the early weeks of its infancy. Delays and continuances by both the prosecution and defense kept pushing back the date of the second trial. Justice kept being delayed and denied. Philip kept in close contact with his former co-workers in the cab industry, and was kept apprised as to the conditions and situations of the drivers. His social life, however, centered around his immediate family and cousins. Upon arrival in the United States, one half of the Fox/Dermer clan put down their roots in South Bend, Indiana, and the other half remained in Chicago. Marion Fox was the eldest child of Baruch Dermer and his wife Raisa. Max Fox was the only member of his family to come to the United States. South Bend became a favorite place to visit when the weather permitted.

Jack, who was the more impetuous and free-wheeling of the Fox brothers, decided at the age of twenty in 1923 to take a bride. He met a beautiful young woman named Faye Saletko, who had been a resident of the Marks Nathan Jewish Orphanage for several years.

The circumstances that placed Fay and her three brothers in this Jewish institution for orphaned children were bizarre. In an instant, the lives of this normal family were changed forever. The Saletko family occupied a small apartment on a commercial street on the West Side of Chicago. Below the apartment was a stable that housed a variety of equine power belonging to the local horse and wagon peddlers.

Late one afternoon on a hot summer day, a fire erupted in the stable below. Its origin was never determined. The raging inferno made the rescue of Mother Saletko and her four children extremely difficult. Thanks to the tireless efforts of neighbors and firemen, Mrs. Saletko and her children were finally extricated from the charred ruins of their home. The trauma of the fire and the rescue suddenly took a toll on the sanity of Mrs. Saletko. She was carried from the burning building screaming that her children had perished in that horrific conflagration. Her mind had snapped and no amount of assurances from family, friends or the authorities could convince her otherwise. Even the very presence of her children did nothing to diminish her screaming anguish. From the moment of the rescue to the end of her days, she never acknowledged her offspring and was totally convinced that they no longer existed.

She was placed in a mental institution to live out her remaining years totally devoid of any knowledge of her past. Visitation by members of her family never drew any sign of recognition from her. After brief one-sided visits they would leave dejected and forlorn. Slowly, all visits stopped. Her end came years later of natural causes. She never regained touch with reality. When she died, the institution which had housed this hapless soul, determining that she had no known relatives, had her buried in a Potters Field. All efforts by her children and grandchildren to find her grave have been unsuccessful.

In the weeks and months following the disastrous fire, Mr. Saletko made a valiant effort to maintain his family, but the odds were against him, and he was forced to place his children in the local Jewish orphanage. It was while residing there that Fay met her future husband.

On May 30th, Memorial Day, 1923, a certain chain of events occurred in Philip's life that was to change his future. Plans had been made by his friends and him to meet early in the morning to attend a picnic at one of the local parks. However, the virtue and the flaw that were unique to Philip's character caused him to miss the appointed hour of departure. This virtue was one of pride in his appearance. It was his hallmark during his lifetime. The flaw, however, was that, in his desire to achieve the ultimate in grooming and attire, he went beyond the norm, and this resulted in his lack of punctuality, much to the chagrin of his family and friends.

Not long before, Philip's brother-in-law Sam Kreiter had mentioned to him a beautiful young Jewish immigrant girl rooming at his sister's house. It seemed to Philip that as long as he missed his rendezvous with his friends, this would be a perfect opportunity to meet this attractive young lady. Satisfied by his appearance in the mirror, he proceeded to meet his life's future mate.

CHAPTER EIGHT

Bella Leibovitz was a beautiful girl and the serenity of their first meeting belied the harshness of her earlier years. She had made the crossing to these shores three years previously in 1920, at the age of fifteen, not wanting to come here, not wanting to leave her mother alone with the burdensome chore of raising her younger brothers and sisters. Her mother was a recent widow. Bella's father had died of influenza while in the Romanian army, just a few years earlier. Bella's job at home as the oldest of seven children was to relieve some of the pressures of daily living, while her mother plied her trade as a seamstress. The small rural Romanian town where they lived was her safe haven, and she did not want to leave it.

Persuaded by her mother, and reassured by her father's two brothers, who were living in America, she boarded the train in Botosani and headed toward her future. Fear and trepidation caused her to leave the train in Bucharest to return home. Convinced that this was the very best move for her oldest child, and the best future for at least one of her children, Chaya Frima was able to placate the fears of her daughter and eventually persuaded her to get back on the train. After settling down for the long journey, she made the acquaintance of several girls also going to America. Their friendship made the trip for Bella a more endurable one, despite her ongoing homesickness.

Bella and her new friends had to part company in Paris. The other girls had to proceed to Marseilles, France, and Bella was going to Amsterdam, Holland. Bella sailed for Montreal, Canada, which was to be her point of entry into the New World. As she traveled down the St. Lawrence River, the strangeness of this new land and the language problems she encountered revived all the apprehensions she had experienced on her leaving home.

Once again Bella found herself on a train, but this time the destination was Chicago, and her journey's end. She was met at the station by her two uncles, who welcomed her with open arms. She settled in at the home of her uncle Willy, his wife and two daughters. Work became the primary occupier of her time. Earning a living to support herself was only a small part of her goal. She contributed a portion of her salary to her uncle's household, and the remaining amount she sent dutifully to her mother, brothers and sisters. Her Uncle Willy had procured employment for her at a local laundry where the hours were long and the work tedious. The girls working there all fit the same mold; they were all immigrants from various parts of the world, and communicated in a variety of languages. Several nights a week she attended public school to learn English and the customs of the United States.

Her days and nights were full, but loneliness for her family never left. Guilt and self-recriminations for leaving them were hard to overcome, despite reassurances from her uncles that this was her mother's wish, and that she had done the right thing. As the days started to pass, maturity and loveliness embraced her features. This loveliness and the attention paid to her by her doting uncle, became a festering sore between Willy and his harping wife. The constant haranguing by her jealous aunt proved to be too much for Bella, and after a little over a year, she moved to her Uncle Isadore's in the Humboldt Park section of Chicago.

Uncle "Izzy," as he was affectionately known, was a stately gentleman and had the appearance of a banker or a Wall Street financier. He and his wife Ida and their three children became Bella's new family. Hart Schaffner & Marx, the clothing manufacturer, became her new employer. Sewing linings and attaching pockets to men's pants was hardly an attractive prospect for the future of this homesick girl of seventeen. Her cousin Sadie, who was close in age to Bella, gave her the companionship she needed to prevent her from slipping into the melancholy state that always stood close at hand, ready to overwhelm her spirit.

Frugality became the watchword for Bella, both out of necessity and strategy, and it was a theme of life that she retained from that point on. Out of necessity she had to survive, but the strategy she had planned was to save enough of her salary in order to afford the return ticket home, or possibly have one or two of her siblings come to America to join her. Every morning she walked the one mile distance to work, and at the end of the day, she trekked the longer distance to her night school classes. She considered the carfare she saved the equivalent of earning that much more money. Her English grammar and knowledge improved with each passing day.

After turning eighteen, the age of female consent in the United States, Bella decided it was time to find the independence and privacy of a mature young woman. The year 1923 did not find single young ladies taking their own apartments, but rather renting a room in a respectable home. Tillie Dorman's home on the West Side was located further from her job and this put a crimp in her savings plan, for she was now forced to ride the Chicago streetcars. This little setback to her finances, she concluded, was well worth the price of her new found independence.

CHAPTER NINE

Whether it was Humboldt Park, Halsted and Maxwell Streets or the West Side, life did not change for the Jewish settler. These neighborhoods were interchangeable in style, custom, and religious practice. Synagogues, grocery stores, meat markets and small specialty shops were easily found in all three neighborhoods. Door to door salesmen known as "custom peddlers" and horse and buggy vendors brought shopping to one's door. All purchases other than for one's daily needs were made at small department stores in the area, or led one to the Bargain Capital of the World, Maxwell Street, the world's largest outdoor market. One always received a bargain on Maxwell Street. If, when one arrived home, one found that the purchase also possessed quality along with the savings, that customer considered himself or herself a lucky and talented shopper.

The phenomena of the open air market of Maxwell Street was the blending of aromas, throngs of people and the continuous din of price hagglers, hustlers and merchant hawkers touting their wares either in their native tongues or in broken, recently learned street English. Having once experienced this cacophony of sounds and smells, one preserved this memory forever.

Free concerts in the park, live Yiddish theater and small movie houses just getting a foothold in the entertainment world became places of diversion from the everyday chore of eking out a living in this Promised Land. Books, periodicals, daily newspapers and pamphlets were available in every mother tongue of every immigrant to land on these shores. Burial societies, workers groups and other fraternal organizations were brought over from the Old World and immediately established in the respective enclaves. Life in the main did not change much from the old country to here, except for the air of freedom and the absence of the pogroms the Jewish immigrants once suffered.

Craziness entered the twenties with a bang. Fads and stunts of all descriptions filled the news. By late 1923 and early 1924, it was reaching its peak. Dance marathons were being held all over the country, and one couple in particular, from Chicago, kept dancing and shuffling for 3,327 consecutive hours. Shipwreck Kelly was sitting on top of a flagpole above a theater in New Jersey, setting a new record for this unique stunt. After the discovery of the tomb of Egyptian Pharaoh Tutankhamen by British archaeologist Howard Carter, the King Tut craze kicked in and people were buying and designing anything Egyptian, including clothes, jewelry, furniture, make-up and hair styles. The oriental game of mah-jongg in its own peculiar way helped the economy of Chicago. Having originated and being manufactured in China, the game's unbelievable acceptance in the United States caused a shortage of calf-shinbones, from which the mah-jongg tiles were made. It was not long before the Chinese manufacturers began importing the shinbones from the Chicago slaughterhouses. The crossword puzzle was created and became a permanent fixture in America's newspapers.

Jazz music, syncopated rhythms and the blues, emanating from the South, were the grease that lubricated the antics of the freewheeling twenties. The twenties also gave rise to the big bands of Paul Whiteman and his Orchestra, Fletcher Henderson and Duke Ellington. George Gershwin's "Rhapsody in Blue," introduced in 1924, became the most played American composition ever. Southern jazz bands were migrating north from New Orleans and Memphis, and finding a more than welcome home in Chicago. Pianos and sheet music filled the parlors of the wealthier homes.

CHAPTER TEN

The scene was idyllic and extremely pleasing to Philip upon his arrival at the home of Tillie Dorman. Bella was swaying gently on the porch swing in the warm sunshine of that delightful Memorial Day morning. Their eyes met, and the magic we know as love began its chemistry. They easily conversed in Yiddish, and discovered the commonality of thoughts between them.

It was the beginning of a whirlwind courtship that lasted just over three months. Dating in the Americanized version of the Yiddish culture and customs, they attended picnics, parties and social events within the family circle. Speakeasies, gin mills and the jazz halls that so abundantly occupied places in almost every neighborhood of Chicago were never the social attraction of Philip and Bella. Philip's younger brother Jack, however, and his recent bride of six months, Faye, appeared more suited to the Flapper scenes that permeated Chicago night life.

Labor Day, September 2, 1923, ended the courtship, but started their life's journey together. Their wedding on that day was filled with hope and promise, and was celebrated at the family home at 1618 South Turner Avenue. Relatives, friends and neighbors alike enjoyed the traditional Jewish wedding food, and the *klezmer* music that wafted through the warm evening air. This occasion of pleasure and happiness, however great, was not enough for Philip to erase the constant thought of the impending second trial and the near disastrous results of the first one from his mind. Unknown to Philip at this time, strong forces were at work in the personae of Benjamin Samuels, George Barrett and other minions of John Hertz and the Yellow Cab Company. Along with their good friends in the State's Attorney's office, they pushed for the implementation of a second trial, hopefully one with a guilty verdict.

Philip and Bella's honeymoon was nonexistent, for the funds were lacking, and the serious business of setting up housekeeping began the next morning. The memory of the festivities of the nuptials of the previous evening faded rapidly as Philip and Bella set up their mini-apartment in the front bedroom of Max and Marion's flat. As was the custom of the day, Philip's brother Jack and his wife Faye occupied the other bedroom in the same apartment. Each new offspring was easily absorbed into the family four-flat.

April of 1924 found Bella and Philip expecting their first child. Bella remained close to the home on Turner Avenue during her confinement, helping her mother-in-law keep the home in order and preparing meals for the other family members as they went about earning a living and attending public school. The bakery business was grueling for Max and Marion, and each married child and spouse helped as much as he or she could, in between their other obligations. On the nineteenth of April, Bella gave birth to her first child at Mount Sinai Hospital. They named him Edward, in memory of Bella's father.

Funds continued to be scarce, and the overcrowded situation on Turner Avenue would not soon be alleviated. Philip continued working as a plumber. The other children of Max and Marion went about their occupations as well. Sam Kreiter, Pauline's husband, was a tailor, as was Sam Geltner, who was married to the second oldest daughter, Fannie. Jack worked at a variety of jobs trying to earn a living, while his wife, Faye, worked as a secretary. The two youngest sisters, Bertha and Rose, attended school part-time and then worked in the bakery the rest of the day. The remaining days of 1924 raced by and Bella found herself once again pregnant. The baby was due to arrive around her own twentieth birthday.

As Bella's due date was approaching, Philip was confronted by a dilemma. Being a staunch union man at this point in his life, he could not bring himself to let his second child be born in a hospital where an addition was under construction by non-union workers. Scab labor was being employed by the general contractor at Mount Sinai Hospital and the picket lines were set. The decision to bypass Mount Sinai and have the baby at the Frances Willard Maternity Hospital was made and Bella delivered their second child, a baby girl named Esther Florence, on May 16, 1925.

Working as a plumber in early 1925, in the days before plastic pipe, copper tubing and automatic and electrified tools, was physically taxing on the body. This occupation either built you up or broke you down; Philip developed a fine muscular physique. Bathtubs and lavatories were made of porcelain-coated cast iron, which were extremely heavy. Threading and cutting of lead pipes were done manually, digging of trenches and holes to install soil pipe was done by hand, and sweating and wiping of lead joints required great dexterity and physical endurance. You earned your salary by the sweat of your brow and the strength of your muscles. He worked long hours during the day and then went home to his young wife and two children, exhausted from the day's toil.

At what point in time Philip told Bella about his previous activities on behalf of the Checker Taxi Company and the terrible situation he found himself in now, we will never know. The second trial was scheduled to begin just one month after the birth of their second child. The news had to be devastating for this young mother of twenty years of age. Being a young immigrant in a strange country was in itself a frightening experience, but now it became compounded with this dreadful oncoming ordeal. To face the immediate future with two very young children, Bella had to summon all her reserve strength and fortitude.

CHAPTER ELEVEN

During the early 1920s, the strike-torn labor unions were dealt a severe blow by Federal District Judge Kenesaw Mountain Landis, who presided in Chicago. Negotiations between the labor unions and the construction moguls had broken down, and the problem had been brought to federal court to be resolved. At the time of the suit, the construction workers were earning $.95 per hour. They were pushing for a dime an hour increase and better working conditions. The construction company owners refused to budge. Judge Landis, after listening to the pros and cons of this case, issued the following opinion: "No man who works with his hands is worth more than $1.00 an hour." The irony of this decision, was that several months after his utterance of this brilliant statement, Judge Landis, resigned his office of Federal Judge, and took the job as Commissioner of Baseball for $50,000.00 a year.

As shameful as this statement was, the second part of his ruling, which became effective in 1925, was to have wider reaching ramifications. He ruled that the construction owners could hire other workers, whether they belonged to the unions or not. Terms of all contracts between the owners and unions, prohibiting the hiring of non-union workers, were therefore illegal.

Accomplishing nothing, but managing to fan the flames of an already smoldering labor situation, this ruling touched off a major conflagration, and 1925 became known as the year of the "Landis Awards Men." "Scab" labor, as the non-union workers were called, were being hired by management to replace union workers at a lower wage. Counting on the court for protection proved to be a fatal mistake for the non-union worker. They were attacked, beaten, and even murdered by the unemployed desperate union workers. Bodies were thrown from the upper floors of tall buildings, and the sound of gunshots rang out at most job locations. Sabotage on new high rises under construction was commonplace. Soil stacks and drainage pipes were filled with concrete rendering them useless. Wiring was purposely crossed to cause small electrical fires. Pandemonium reigned at the construction site.

This social upheaval was not the only headline grabbing the reading public. Darwin's "theory of evolution" was now on trial in a small court house in Dayton, Tennessee. John T. Scopes was accused of teaching Darwin's theory on the Origin of Man in defiance of a court order. This was the start of the famous "Monkey Trial." Highlighting the trial and fueling the headlines were the two most famous attorneys of their time.

William Jennings Bryan was the prosecutor in the case. He was nominated for the presidency of the United States three times and defeated all three times. He was Secretary of State under President Wilson but resigned due to a conflict with the President. Many considered Bryan to be the greatest fiery orator and litigator on the side of Christian beliefs, but this case came at the twilight of his career. His opponent, the attorney for the defense, was the most famous lawyer of them all, Clarence Darrow, of Chicago. Somewhere near the end of the trial, Bryan volunteered to take the stand so he could expound on his fundamentalist beliefs. He was mercilessly cross-examined by Darrow. The strain was too great for Bryan and he died three days after the trial ended. Bryan won the case but lost his life.

CHAPTER TWELVE

Philip's second trial finally became a reality in the June 1925 term of the Criminal Court of Cook County. Unlike the murder of Skirven and the first trial, this second trial did not even make the papers. The world had moved on; more sensational events filled the headlines. The attorneys representing both defendants at this time were Michael J. Ahern and Elwyn E. Long, two prestigious attorneys from downtown Chicago. The presiding judge was William N. Gemmill.

William A. Rittenhouse was the prosecutor and opened the trial with a reading of the charges and indictments. Ahern and Long countered with a motion for dismissal on the grounds of the involuntary confessions. The motion was denied. Rittenhouse then called the prosecution witnesses to the occurrence.

They testified: "that the shot that killed Skirven was fired from a dark touring car about one o'clock in the morning; that the car was moving slowly at the time the shots were fired; and that it proceeded north at an increased speed after the shooting." The next witness was a Chauncey Scandiff. He testified that "shortly after 1:00 o'clock in the morning, he was driving a Yellow cab south on Kedzie Avenue toward Twelfth Street (Roosevelt Road); that at Arthington Street, a black touring car approached him at a rapid rate of speed; that the driver seemed to be preparing to turn at Arthington Street and cut over toward him, so that he thought there was going to be a collision; that both cars slowed down so that when the touring car passed him it was travelling [*sic*] about 15 miles an hour and he was travelling [*sic*] about 8 miles an hour; that he glanced into the touring car, and saw Charles Goldstein, who was indicted along with Fox and Steuben [*sic*], sitting by the side of the driver; that he continued south on Kedzie Avenue to the Yellow Cab station, and found Skirven lying on the floor with a bullet wound in his chest."

Robert Stamm was the next to testify, and he stated that "before midnight of June 8th, he saw Goldstein, Fox, Steuben [*sic*], Mogley and Podolsky at the Paulina Street Checker Taxi garage; that Goldstein, in the presence of Fox and Steuben [*sic*], asked him to go with them to kill some Yellow Cab drivers; that he refused to go, but that all of the five persons named got into a Checker taxicab and drove away." He testified further "that Fox saw him subsequent to the murder, and asked him not to go to the courthouse and testify against him; that he told him he (Stamm) would do his best not to be there; that Fox asked him to meet him the next day, and he would get him a job with the Checker Taxi Company."

Clement C. Peter testified that "he was employed as a Yellow Cab chauffeur on June 9th; that he was at the station at Logan Square about 2:30 a.m.; that a car, which appeared to him to be a Hudson touring car, drove by the station slowly; that there were five men in the car; and that they fired a number of shots at him as they drove by; that one of the men in the back seat was Stuben."

Witnesses Peter Hanson and David J. Brown repeated their testimony from the first trial, regarding the suspicious movement of the five men around Brown's Pool Hall and Restaurant and the discovery later on of the weapons found behind the pool hall in the alley.

The prosecution ended the parade of witnesses with a Samuel Miller. He testified that "he was, on June 9th, 1921, floor man and manager of the Paulina Street Checker Taxi garage and that Stuben and Fox were drivers who worked out of that garage. He identified one of the guns found at the rear of Brown's Pool Hall as the property of Stuben and another one of them as the property of Fox." He testified further that "he saw Fox and Stuben after they were released on bail, and that Fox in the latter part of July 1921; at the Paulina Street garage [*sic*]; that he talked with him about the charges against him; and that Fox said there would be nothing to the trial; then he testified that he told Fox, that he did not think much of anybody who done a thing like that; and that Fox replied, 'Well, there is no use in saying anything; it is not going to bring him back to life.'" Miller then testified that "he saw Stuben two or three days later at the same place; that he asked him when he got out of jail; and that Stuben replied that he got out the same time as Fox. In discussing the trial, Miller asked Stuben why he went out and shot up the town, and Stuben replied that he had a bee in his bonnet, from an argument he had at the Sherman

House with Yellow Cab drivers, and that one of them tossed a brick through the window of his cab, and another gave him a black eye, and that he went out to get even with them."

On cross-examination, the veracity and machinations of some of the prosecution witnesses became very apparent. Their motives for their testimony came rapidly to the surface. This is the way the cross-examination went. Scandiff admitted that he did not reveal to anyone for more than a year after the murder that he had seen Goldstein in the black touring car fleeing from the scene of the shooting. He did not appear at the coroner's inquest, nor before the grand jury, nor did he testify at the first trial. On cross-examination, Miller admitted that "he left the employ of the Checker Taxi Company in September, 1921, and that he, Miller, had since been employed as an investigator by the Yellow Cab Company; and that he was among those being questioned at the State's Attorney's office June 9, 1921, and that he was in that office from 3 o'clock in the afternoon until 7 o'clock the next morning and that he, Miller, knew something about the murder at that time, but that he told those in charge of the investigation that he did not; that he did not testify at the coroner's inquest nor before the grand jury; that the first time he revealed the information that he had regarding the ownership of the guns and the conversations he had with Fox and Stuben was after he had trouble with the Checker Taxi company and left its employ; and that thereafter he went to an officer of the Yellow Cab company and gave him the information about the guns and the statements. Stamm stated on cross-examination that the first time he told the story about seeing the five persons indicted leave in an automobile, with the declaration that they were going to kill Yellow Cab drivers, was when Miller came to see him about the matter after the jury had failed to agree at the first trial."

At this juncture in the trial, the total ineptness of the defense attorneys at the first trial, whether intentional or unintentional, becomes obvious to those who read these transcripts. The very fact that all three witnesses, Scandiff, Miller and Stamm, had a selfish ax to grind, collectively and individually, was never challenged.

Scandiff and Miller appeared to have sold their so-called information for employment at the Yellow Cab Company, clearly a year after the first trial and their troubles with the Checker Cab Company. They apparently never considered going to the police or the proper authorities first. Stamm also never came forward for at least a year after the first trial, until he was solicited by the new investigator for Yellow Cab, Mr. Miller. One can only assume that the payoffs were made and that Fox and Stuben had been set-up to take the fall. How high up this arrangement went, after so many years have elapsed, is very hard to determine.

With all the statements and conclusions coming forth from the trial transcripts, appeal hearings, and pardon hearings, had Fox and Stuben been put on the stand to refute and contradict the obvious lies and fabrications by the prosecution witnesses, the outcome of the second trial would have been entirely different. Inasmuch as the incriminating circumstances and statements stood in the record undisputed, the jury felt justified in giving the uncontradicted testimony of the witnesses for the state full credit. The jury felt the evidence warranted the verdict. After a rather short deliberation, the jury returned a verdict of guilty of murder, and fixed their punishment at life imprisonment in the penitentiary at Joliet, Illinois. On the 10th day of July 1925, the Honorable William N. Gemmill sentenced each to prison for the term of his natural life.

The fate of the other three defendants, Goldstein, Mogley and Podolsky? They were granted a separate trial on December 10, 1923, which happened to fall between the first and second trials of Fox and Stuben.

William A. Rittenhouse, who was the Assistant State's Attorney who originally prosecuted Fox and Stuben, entered a motion of *nolle proseque*, meaning broadly "lack of evidence." Having been unable to obtain a confession from Goldstein, Mogley and Podolsky, the state would have to rely solely on circumstantial evidence, and Rittenhouse felt that the circumstantial evidence was insufficient to secure a conviction.

Incredible as it now seems, almost seventy-five years after the fact, the identical circumstantial evidence that Rittenhouse felt was too weak to go to trial with against Goldstein, Mogley and Podolsky, was strong enough for the State's Attorney's office to go forward and proceed with a second trial of Fox and Stuben. Once again it appears that the evil forces were at work against them. This cabal of legal eagles from the State's Attorney's office and the Yellow Cab Company once more easily had their way with the judicial system in Cook County.

The witness Robert Stamm, who gave the most damaging testimony in the second trial, had a most interesting background. At the time he gave his testimony, he was under indictment in the Criminal Court of Cook County himself, and later after the second trial, twice pleaded guilty to the crime of manslaughter. The second irony attached to this witness was that he was represented by attorney John F. Tyrell, a lawyer who was then associated with attorney George F. Barrett, former judge of the Circuit Court, and at the time of the arrests, the chief legal counsel for the Yellow Cab Company. He is the same George F. Barrett who supervised the unlawful inquisition of Fox and Stuben, and the former law partner of State's Attorney Robert E. Crowe. The stench of tainted testimony and bad legal decisions by the defense attorneys reeked throughout the courthouse.

Following the glaring errors of the defense attorneys, one can surmise the chicanery that was indulged in by the several parties involved in the eventual outcome. Peace found its way between the warring factions of the taxi industry. It appeared that the two strongest combatants, John Hertz of Yellow Cab and Mike Sokol of Checker reached an accommodation.

Their agreement must have been reached sometime between the first trial of 1922 and the second trial of 1925. In spite of the release of the other three alleged occupants of the suspect vehicle, Fox and Stuben were forced to stand trial a second time. It did not take too much pressure from Hertz to convince State's Attorney Crowe to proceed. Now that peace had come between them and things had quieted down, Hertz and Sokol let the law of Chicago finish off the two sacrificial lambs. It was an easy sacrifice of two insignificant cab drivers, at least in their minds.

CHAPTER THIRTEEN

Will the certainty of a reversal by the Illinois Supreme Court of the conviction, as predicted by the defense attorneys, come true, or end up in a cruel hoax as the other two trials before? The appeals to the Illinois Supreme Court were immediately filed and now the waiting for a decision began anew.

Following the guilty verdict, Philip's and Morris's bonds were revoked and they were remanded into the custody of the Sheriff of Cook County awaiting the results of their appeal. Hoping for a turn-over of the conviction and a new trial to take place, Philip and his new attorney, Edgar J. Cook, were determined to place Philip on the stand to tell the truth of what happened, and refute the false testimony of the prosecution witnesses. The Illinois Supreme Court did not take up the matter of the appeal for Fox and Stuben until December 16, 1925. Having processed the papers, and hoping for the best, Philip continued to languish in Cook County jail through the remainder of 1925.

With Philip's first experience of incarceration, a new problem was created for Bella and Marion. Philip refused to eat the non-kosher food given to him by the Sheriff's deputies. His health became a major concern. To solve the crisis, Bella became determined to bring him one kosher meal at lunch time every day. Marion came home at noon from her duties at the bakery to take care of Esther and Edward. Bella would pack up the meal, and then board three consecutive street cars to reach the old county jail. Philip ate with gusto and was able to sustain himself on that single delicious meal, brought to him daily by his loving and caring wife.

The Jewish population of the West Side of Chicago kept swelling in numbers. Hebrew schools and synagogues were springing up every day. Douglas Boulevard, from its beginning at Sacramento Boulevard to its right angle turn emptying into Independence Boulevard, was considered an upscale section of the West Side. It became the focal point of synagogues and assorted Jewish centers. Yiddish was the second and sometimes first language of the pedestrians walking this beautiful tree lined street. Manicured lawns and flower gardens added to the color and fragrance of this Yiddish thoroughfare. Fumes and noise from the automobiles and the Chicago Motor Coach Company buses were all that marred its serenity and aroma. Jewish folk heroes of the future, in every field of endeavor, were being born in the tumultuous twenties in Chicago. Scholars, entertainers, sports figures and famous politicians were being reared in the American-Yiddish culture of the West Side.

Movies began to be the great escape from realism in the twenties, and 1925 was no exception. Harold Lloyd was the acrobatic comic of the silent films, and Charlie Chaplin started his climb to celluloid immortality as the "Little Tramp." Dorothy Gish and her sister, Lillian, were luminous stars, acting together or separately in the silent films. Rudolph Valentino plucked at the heart strings and imagination of both young and old female patrons, while youngsters thrilled to the western antics of such stars as Buck Jones, Hoot Gibson and Tom Mix.

Fifty million listeners were tuned into their favorite radio programs by 1925. This new medium of mass communication was proliferating at the rate of 1.5 million new radios being purchased a year. Rudy Vallee, known as the "Vagabond Lover," was one of radio's first singing stars, and his nasal tone was immediately recognized by his millions of female fans. Ed Wynn was the top comic of his day; while two Chicago vaudevillians, Freeman Gosden and Charles Correll, created a show that ran for decades, and was known as "Amos 'n' Andy." David Sarnoff founded the National Broadcasting Company (N.B.C.), partly based on his experience as a young wireless operator, relaying the famous distress signals from the sinking Titanic back in 1912, and forwarding them on to a stunned nation.

Originating in the Maxwell Street section, and then relocating just down the street on Ogden Avenue, one block from Max Fox's bakery, was a cigar company known as United States Cigars. Its owners were a family by the name of Paley. From this humble beginning came the seed money for their son William S. Paley to purchase a near bankrupt chain of 16 radio stations and create the Columbia Broadcasting System (C.B.S.). The battle of these two communication giants for the listening audience was just beginning.

Diversion from the movies and the radio, as new and exciting as they were, were still not enough to erase the constant worry of Philip and Bella, and the entire Fox clan, from the possibility of the failure of the Illinois Supreme Court to reverse the jury's verdict in the second trial. The idea of possibly serving out the imposed sentence of the court was abhorrent. Bella suffered in silence and prayed daily for the best possible outcome. Not lacking for moral support from his family, Philip counted the slowly passing days until the Illinois Supreme Court handed down its ruling. The sweltering Chicago summer faded as Philip and Bella passed their second anniversary. Rosh Hashana and Yom Kippur gave way to the fall season. At long last, December 16, 1925, brought forth the momentous decision from the Supreme Court.

The cold of the coming winter could not have been more chilling than the final words of the majority opinion: "The judgement of the criminal court is affirmed, appeal denied." Shock waves were generated through the family, and the news brought a feeling of total despair. Philip and Morris were to commence serving their sentences at Stateville Penitentiary right after the start of the new year of 1926. They were to remain in the custody of the Cook County Sheriff through the holiday season. On January 8, 1926, they entered Stateville Penitentiary at Joliet; Philip Fox as Prisoner #329 and Morris Stuben as Prisoner #330.

Depression and despair filled the heart and thoughts of prisoner #329 as he entered the cavernous anteroom of this inhospitable penal institution. At the same time that Philip was undergoing his indoctrination process, his attorneys were feverishly preparing another petition to the Illinois Supreme Court for a rehearing. Philip's new counsel realized that the legal strategy of his predecessors had been a gross miscalculation and now he was scrambling to try to correct it. It had become apparent that the previous attorneys, under the payroll of the Checker Taxi Association and its president, Mike Sokol, did not always have the best interests of their clients uppermost in their minds.

Ignoring the trial errors committed by both the court and the prosecution, the defense attorneys based their first appeal to the

Illinois Supreme Court solely on the question of voluntary and involuntary confessions. Obvious errors that were grounds for reversal were not enumerated for the high court to deliberate. Several rules of law were left to the discretion of the jury, when in fact rules of law should only be decided by the presiding judge. Testimony and statements by several prosecution witnesses were total distortions and fabrications of the truth. They were never challenged.

Various precedents on the question of voluntary and involuntary confessions date back to 1783. Since that first clear expression in the *Warickshalls* case in 1783, the law has taken on several different interpretations of voluntary and involuntary confessions. According to the opinion of the majority of the Illinois Supreme Court ruling in this case, it did not matter how the confession was obtained, even through duress and battery, as long as the final results of the confession be proven as truthful. However, the precedent of the past 150 years of Illinois Supreme Court rulings has determined that confessions obtained involuntarily either through mental duress or severe physical punishment are not to be allowed in evidence.

Several of the glaring errors pointed out by the majority opinion which the justices pointed out could have reversed their ruling were: (1) the attorneys for the defense never laid the proper foundation for the admission in evidence of the notes showing the examination of Fox and Stuben; (2) the defense attorneys' motion for a separate trial for Philip Fox, where he would have been prosecuted strictly on circumstantial evidence, as his confession was never allowed to be entered, was filed too late and was denied; his fate now was forever tied to Stuben's, even though he was not mentioned in Stuben's confession; (3) the defense also failed to complain and note that after deciding that the confession of Stuben was voluntary, the court by instructions resubmitted the question to the jury. This was totally improper. In one of their concluding statements, the majority says, "There are many things revealed on the cross examinations, which seriously affect the credit to be given the testimony of the prosecution witnesses. If their testimony did not stand in the record wholly uncontradicted, there might be some basis for the argument that their testimony was unworthy." This was the single greatest error of all committed by their defense attorneys in not permitting Fox and Stuben to take the stand to refute the obvious lies.

Judge John Duncan's dissenting opinion went beyond his brilliant legal minority view. He reveals his emotions in his declaration of outrage at the very basic civil rights denied Fox and Stuben, and the total trampling on their human rights by every person of the State's Attorney's office, police and so-called associates involved in the arrest, illegal incarceration, and brutal interrogation.

Not apprising the two defendants of their constitutional rights immediately upon their arrest and interrogation was the first critical error by the prosecution. According to Judge Duncan, Fox and Stuben should not have been the only ones charged with criminal conduct. He stated further: "[T]he defendants were literally kidnaped by the police and forcibly taken to the State's Attorney's office, and there held, and then were compelled to submit to examinations, and to threats, abuses, and assaults by the police, of the most contemptible character, to compel them to confess, without the aid or advice of friendly counsel. No State's Attorney has any lawful authority or right to engage in such proceedings. It is not only a violation of the ethics of his profession, if such a proceeding is indulged in for the illegal purpose of extorting or forcing a confession from the defendants, it is a willful and deliberate violation of his constitutional oath as an attorney at law, and as a State's Attorney. It is also a grave violation of the constitutional rights of the defendants. This is also true of every assistant who willfully and knowingly participates in such an unlawful proceeding, and is equally true of every licensed lawyer who participates. The constitutional oath in this country is still binding upon the lawyer and public officer as it ever has been, in a legal and constitutional sense. No officer or attorney should disregard his oath and adopt the theory of the faddists or supposed reformers, who preach that the way to convict criminals is to commit crime in trying them and to disregard utterly the law and the constitution in criminal trials."

Judge Duncan continued with his closing statements: "The police officers who participated in the beating and maltreating of these prisoners, were guilty of the most cowardly assault and battery that it is possible to commit. It is the criminal assault and battery upon a helpless and disarmed prisoner, whom it was their duty to treat humanely and to have them promptly committed to jail, pending the investigation by a grand jury or coroner's jury or some other legal body. The defendants had a right to a speedy and legal investigation, and to the advice of legal counsel, if indicted by a grand jury for crime. Every person who knowingly aids, assists, advises, or abets such criminal assault is equally guilty, with the police who actually committed the same. The police officers are guilty of a willful and deliberate violation of their oath of office, if such assaults were committed to compel confessions.

"The court should have passed on the legal evidence before it, bearing on these alleged confessions, and in doing so should have considered the interest of all parties who testified on the question, and have suppressed the confession on the evidence submitted. The people have not made the proper effort to obtain a real and true investigation of the question whether or not the confessions were voluntarily made, this record shows that such is the case, and the judgement should be reversed and the case remanded for another trial."

These emotional words by Judge John Duncan, would become very significant for Fox and Stuben a few years later in time. Vastly different interpretations of evidence and the laws pertaining to them, still remain the check and balance in our judicial system.

CHAPTER FOURTEEN

With the immediate revocation of his bond upon the guilty verdict in the second trial, the income of Philip and Bella dropped to zero. Being held in county jail until the decision in the appeal to the Illinois Supreme Court, Philip could no longer work. Bella could not go and seek work either, due to the very young ages of her children.

To compensate her in-laws for their stay in the apartment, Bella undertook all phases of the daily upkeep of not only the apartment but the building as well. This included the very menial job of scrubbing floors on her hands and knees and maintenance of the two hallways of the residence. Whatever task was asked of her, by anyone in the building, Bella performed it at her best, with no objections or resistance. The lack of income for Bella and her children became apparent to Jack early in this waiting game. He devised a plan to help her as best he could, without her feeling that she was receiving charity. Every two or three weeks, he would hand her a small check, and tell her it was a loan from the cab drivers until her Philip was released from jail. Whether it was due to a guilty conscience or a deep concern for the welfare of his brother's family, it was readily accepted by her and it helped to restore some dignity to her life and provide for some of the basic needs for her children.

Society does not concern itself with guilt or innocence when it places a stigma or label on a person. Headlines are always much bolder when the news breaks than the printed retraction later on when the truth is known. It was not long before the neighbors forgot the circumstances of the case, but only remembered the present situation of the Fox family of 1618 South Turner Avenue. Their son, husband, brother and father was convicted of a capital crime and was sitting in jail. Acrimony from some of the neighbors began to rear its ugly head. Bella had to endure knowing side-long glances while all the children of the building were reminded that their father and uncle was a jailbird. The rest of the family heard tongue-clucking and offers of pity and sympathy to their plight.

After the appeal was denied in December of 1925, the economic future for Philip's wife and children seemed even bleaker.

Jack, after learning of this negative news, passed this information on to his friends in the cab business. Because they believed so strongly in their innocence and in recognition of the sacrifice Philip and Morris had made on their behalf, the cab drivers decided to hold a fund raiser to benefit Philip's wife and children, and Morris Stuben's wife, Rose, and their two daughters. In 1926, the best event to draw the most people and raise the most money was a dinner-dance. This was the 1920s and dancing was all the rage. The cause was important and the event proved to be very successful. The drivers were able to present to Bella and Rose a check for $1,400 dollars each (equivalent to approximately fourteen thousand dollars based on today's value).

Bella accepted the money with deep humility, and great gratitude toward the drivers who organized the affair and helped to make it such a success. From the onset of her receiving the fourteen hundred dollars, Bella had no intention of spending the money on herself or her children. When her mother-in-law arrived home from her day at the bakery, Bella extended the check to her as payment for their stay in the apartment. Marion, known for her generosity and concern, refused the money, and insisted that Bella put the money in the bank for their future needs. Marion, always optimistic, and with her deep belief that her son would be found innocent and released one day, knew that the money would be needed to start a new life. During the ensuing three years after the first fund raiser, the drivers held several more to continue to offer support to the two families.

Bella's strength of character never allowed her to take the fourteen hundred dollars along with her two young children back to the more familiar atmosphere of her mother's home in Romania. It could have easily been accomplished. She still had her passport and fares were reasonable. There she could have awaited the release of her husband and then returned to America. This would have been the normal inclination for a young married woman with two small children and a husband in prison. This idea never entered her mind for several reasons. The first was Marion's continual optimism for Philip's early release, along with her assurances that several forces were at work to hurry the process to achieve that goal. She also would never bring such a burden to her mother, who was trying desperately to survive in her own situation, with all her children and no husband. Bella was of strong resolve, and determined to stay the course.

With still a small glimmer of hope in his heart for a reversal of his sentence pursuant to the petition for rehearing filed on his behalf, Philip tried to settle into prison life. He was assigned to the kitchen detail as his primary duty, in addition to the other jobs required of prisoners. Regimentation of the forced nature of prison was foreign to Philip, and it required all his strength of determination to acclimate to the penal system. The independence and pride that Philip possessed slowly melted into submission and obedience. To know that he was innocent, and yet to be subjected to such punishment, could possibly have been a devastating blow to his psyche, but the counterbalancing thought that his entire family, numerous friends, and former associates were working hard on his behalf, was the safety valve he needed.

Stateville Penitentiary in Joliet, Illinois, on a clear sun-bright day is still a foreboding and sinister edifice. The tall white, 32 feet high limestone walls conclude their imposing height with watchtower crowns on each corner, filled with guards and searchlights maintaining a constant vigil. Large iron gates in front stood as the welcoming committee for incoming prisoners.

The socially accepted principals of dehumanizing people back in the nineteen twenties and thirties were applied by the prisons and the military. However, there was a very distinct difference between the two.

The military services used the same system as the prisons use initially to break down the prisoner's spirit to the lowest common denominator. This was the indoctrination period known as basic training. It was done in order to rebuild them in the mold of militarily correct thinking and training. Phase two was the actual military training, now that the men were more readily adaptable. Phase three was the leadership category, which embraced the training and teaching of the other two phases.

Prisons, to the contrary, up to the middle 1930s, only used the comparable first phase of the military. Their intent was to break down the incoming prisoner, and maintain him in that state, until he was released from custody or died. The rehabilitation phase never existed nor was even thought of until 1935, when classes and visiting teachers were allowed inside the prison walls.

The Illinois State Legislature established the prison system in Illinois barely out of the state's own infancy, by passing a law in 1827 creating the first prison in Alton. The first prisoner to occupy the newly completed prison was a burglar from downstate in 1833. By 1837, there were sixty men housed in this new facility, and by Christmas of 1838, they had their first bona fide prison breakout.

Due to its proximity to Chicago, where most of the prisoners were coming from, Joliet was chosen as the site for a new prison. It was designed and built in a castle-like Gothic style. A request for a new prison was first made in 1886 to alleviate overcrowding in Joliet. The numerous requests were denied until 1907, when the state legislature authorized a new prison built just five miles from Joliet. The initial money for the new prison became available in 1913, and the actual work began in 1917. This was the beginning of Stateville. On the sixty-four acre site, five one-of-a-kind circular structures stand. They are four tiers high and are called "panopticons." Four of the buildings are cell houses and the fifth is a mess hall. The buildings were designed in this fashion, so that one guard could observe an entire cell house. Stateville was officially opened in March of 1925.

It is an oxymoron to refer to a prison as a pleasant place, but compared to the old prison in Joliet, Stateville was a dream to some of the prisoners that got transferred in 1925. One of these prisoners was the infamous Nathan Leopold, who with his friend, Richard Loeb, murdered young Bobby Franks in 1924 to see if they could commit the perfect crime.

Upon his arrival in Stateville, Leopold issued this description: "Above all, the cells were clean and airy. Indeed, it was the cleanliness and airiness that impressed me the most about Stateville as a whole. What a contrast to the grimy, gloomy, forbidding surroundings of the old prison. Here the eye could wander hundreds of yards in one direction before being stopped by the barrier of the prison wall. From my high cell on the fourth gallery, I could look over the walls to the rolling farmland beyond."[1]

When Philip entered Stateville, just nine months after its opening, the cells and other facilities were still in the state of newness, but the administration and penal system inside was just as crooked and corrupt as it had been in the old prison, just five miles away. The period between 1925 and 1932 was marked by violence among inmates, and between inmates and staff. The absence of a strong and capable administration made this period one of the most lawless and violent in the history of Stateville. In 1926, seven inmates took the deputy warden hostage, and stabbed him to death when he refused at knife point to help in their escape. Lack of direction and goals for the prisoners by warden Elmer Greene and his administration was considered the primary cause for this lawlessness. In 1927, 85% of the inmates were idle. If you were politically connected, you served your time with relative ease.

---

[1] James B. Jacobs, *Stateville* (Chicago: The University of Chicago Press, 1977) 15.

CHAPTER FIFTEEN

Philip's work in the prison kitchen kept him fully occupied, as he tried to pass the time as productively as possible. The new, modern (based on 1926 standards) kitchen was a beehive of activity, as the staff prepared and served thousands of meals a day. After completion of his shift, he and the other prisoners marched in line in silence to their cells, where they awaited the following day's routine.

It was just one month after entering prison that Philip received the bad news. On February 5, 1926, the Illinois Supreme Court denied the petition for a rehearing. His hopes for an early release were dashed by the utterance of this single word, "denied." Looming in the future for Philip at this time were just the endless days and nights of loneliness; to be so near Chicago, but yet so distant from his home and family. The prospect of not being with his beautiful young wife, Bella, and helping her to raise their young children, compounded his suffering. The outside world, of which he had been a vibrant part until recently, was now not available to him.

His only contacts with the forbidden fruit of normal life were the visits from his family every second Tuesday, for a brief few hours. They were never permitted to touch or embrace, except for a fleeting moment allowed by the watchful guard stationed nearby. Visiting days were Philip's only lifeline to the real world. It was the time when he learned of the latest news national and local, and the more treasured tidbits of family happenings and gossip. Bella related to him the cute everyday antics of his two growing offspring.

Preparing for the trip to Joliet every second Tuesday was now becoming a hectic routine at 1618 South Turner Avenue. Preparations were supervised by the watchful Marion. Shopping bags of Philip's favorite foods and necessities of life, such as underwear, shaving cream, blades and toothpaste, were filled to capacity. Philip's brother Jack prepared the Pierce-Arrow touring car, which they owned jointly, and had used as a Checker cab earlier, for the one and one-half to two hour ride to Joliet.

Members of the family alternated as to who went to visit. Bella went every time accompanied by Marion and Bella's two children, Edward and Esther, and sometimes one or two of his sisters or the older Kreiter children. The family's love and affection for Philip ran deep, and his incarceration caused them great pain and anguish.

Upon entering the large visitors' room, the family was instructed to sit on one side of the row of long white tables. The prisoners then entered and sat on the opposite side. All bags had been inspected for contraband goods and weapons at the door, and were now allowed to be given to the prisoners. Philip ate with total enjoyment as the quality of prison food did not come close to meeting the pungent and delectable cooking of his mother. He was not able to observe the kosher dietary laws in prison, and so awaited every visiting day with great anticipation. While enjoying this wonderful manna from home, he listened eagerly to all the news. Prior to returning to his cell, Philip distributed the remaining food to some of his fellow prisoners. The hours following the departure of his family proved to be full of melancholy and loneliness.

Time under incarceration moves extremely slowly, and now along with the rehearing denial, despair became Philip's psychological enemy. Questioning if and when he would ever be released remained constantly on his mind. Here behind the intimidating walls of Stateville, at the age of twenty-five, the very early years of adulthood, Philip could not contemplate a very bright future for himself, his wife, and two children.

The rehearing denial, although a devastating blow to the Fox family, only served to stiffen their resolve to work harder for his exoneration and release. They were determined to let no stone go unturned, and no avenue unexplored, in searching for some form of help and pressure to bear against the legal system that was keeping their beloved family member in prison. Philip's brother Jack and his youngest sister Rose redoubled their efforts to try to set their brother free.

Soliciting help from local politicians, such as ward leaders and aldermen, and from the religious leaders of the Jewish community, proved not to be enough clout at this time in Chicago, as the reform minded administration of Mayor William Dever, of the Democratic

Party, was just coming into power. The state government was still controlled by the Republicans under Governor Len Small. Jack and Rose both realized now that it would require a considerable sum of money to hire the most able attorneys to file a petition to the Board of Pardons and Paroles for a hearing. This was the next step in the long appeal process.

How to raise the money became the next pressing problem. Jack and Philip had many loyal friends and associates still working in the taxi industry, as drivers and middle management executives. Jack and Rose brought the plight of Philip and Morris to this nucleus of drivers and executives, and relayed to them their dilemma on how to raise funds to hire the lawyers needed to proceed to the next step.

The drivers remembered the efforts and leadership that Philip and Morris displayed on their behalf during the hellish years of the cab wars, and also remembered with bitterness how the Yellow Cab Company, with the total backing of the corrupt Thompson city hall, tried to prevent them from participating in the lucrative and burgeoning taxi business in Chicago. They pledged their support and money, and thus began a groundswell of financial help by the Checker drivers and independents alike. They raised upwards of $10,000.00, which was a vast sum of money in the year 1926.

Bella was having a hard time coping with Philip's first year of incarceration. Normal childhood diseases contracted by her two young children seemed a lot harder for her to deal with in the absence of her husband. Loneliness for her family in Romania was still with her, and along with her husband in prison, those nights when she was not totally exhausted were becoming almost unbearable. Everyday problems that ordinarily would be easy to overcome became magnified and exaggerated to the point of frustration.

Because of Marion's busy schedule of trying to juggle her work at the bakery and solving the daily problems of her extended family, she gave the appearance of a certain aloofness, which kept Bella at arm's length from her mother-in-law. Max, on the other hand, in his usual kind and considerate way, was able to assuage the hurt feelings of his lonely, young daughter-in-law. Marion and her six offspring were emotional people and more often than not wore their emotions on their collective sleeves. From childhood to adulthood and into their married lives, when one sibling had a problem, it soon became an entire family crisis that had to have a satisfactory resolution as soon as possible.

There was never a dull moment at 1618 South Turner Avenue, as the individual families grew larger with each passing year. By 1926, Sam and Pauline Kreiter had three children, David, Harry and Abe. Sam and Fanny Geltner were raising two children, Ruth and Barry. Philip and Bella's two children, Edward and Esther, were the youngest children in the building. Jack and his wife Faye were still unable to conceive, and the two youngest daughters of Max and Marion, Bertha and Rose, remained single.

CHAPTER SIXTEEN

Sports in 1926 was another area that saw great events and attractions that drew millions of spectators. Jack Dempsey, known as the "Manassa Mauler," one of the world's greatest heavyweight boxers, was coming to the end of his illustrious career. Gene Tunney, who had won the light-heavyweight title while in the army in the first World War, squared-off with Dempsey after a long lay-off period and totally out-boxed him in the "City of Brotherly Love," Philadelphia.

Knute Rockne, the most celebrated coach of Notre Dame football, was weaving his spell over their opponents, and building the legend of this venerable university. The fabled Notre Dame backfield, dubbed " The Four Horsemen" by sportswriter Grantland Rice, along with the dazzling running of Red Grange, the "Galloping Ghost of Illinois," filled the sports pages with incredible football exploits.

Rice, along with Paul Gallico, Ring Lardner and Damon Runyan, were some of the popular sportswriters of this era. It was their brilliant narratives of the sports they reported on that created the legends in every sport of the period. Baseball, football, tennis, golf, boxing and horse racing, each in its own dominion, produced the kings and queens they raised on pedestals to the lofty heights of immortality.

Ford Motor Company, the innovator of the mass produced family auto, was also the pioneer in establishing one of great benefits for the American worker, the "Five Day Work Week." At this same time, International Harvester instituted another of the laboring world's shining jewels, the two weeks paid vacation. A worker earning $2,000 per year was considered part of "Middle Class America." Doctors and lawyers, even as today, were in a higher bracket, averaging $5,000 per year. However, unlike today, doctors made house calls to the sick and infirm.

Once the automobile became accepted, and then affordable, to the average family, America became a mobile, explorative nation. The Lincoln Highway, the country's first coast to coast route, became choked with vehicles and exhaust fumes. Along this 3,400 mile route, sprang up new industries catering to the venturing public. Gas stations, roadside restaurants, souvenir stores and a brand new phenomenon, the roadside motel, were among them. The first established hostelry of this nature was opened in California in 1926, and the word "motel" was added to the American lexicon from that day forward.

Though the general work force in the United States had made considerable gains in the early twenties, organized labor had suffered a number of setbacks by the end of 1926. The miners' union under bushy-eyebrowed, dynamic John L. Lewis, was not gaining the same momentum on working improvements as were some other labor organizations. Theirs was the bottom portion of the American worker. They worked under the most deplorable and unsafe conditions, with some of the lowest remuneration for their backbreaking labor. Farmers across the nation were suffering from high tariffs on their export crops. Bankruptcies became commonplace and small rural communities became ghost towns, as the farmers abandoned the soil to seek work in the industrialized cities. Labor strikes for better wages and conditions were no longer an effective weapon for the organized worker. The courts began issuing injunctions against them, and management hired armed personnel to intervene with the help of the local constabulary. Eight thousand garment workers alone were arrested off the picket lines in New York City. The chasm between the haves and the have-nots grew larger and larger.

CHAPTER SEVENTEEN

This was the outside world in late 1926 in which Philip was not privileged to participate. Nor was he to be aware of the daily experiences and the rapid advancements of society in general, in the high-flying days of life in the 1920s. Confinement usurped the unusual as well as the ordinary things that once comprised his life. Simple pleasures and privileges he once took for granted were now totally denied him. Nature's sunshine in itself had become a rare commodity of life, to enjoy when given the opportunity by his appointed guards.

The *quid pro quo* of politics and the partisan spoils system ran Stateville during the near three year stint of Philip's incarceration. It was not until the Clabaugh commission was formed in 1928 that civil service reform was even considered in the hiring of staff and guards. Governor Len Small was still receiving kickbacks from his appointees to settle judgments against him arising from his own personal lawsuits in Waukegan. Philip tried to maintain his mental equilibrium during this unstable period of life at Stateville. The harder the system tried to drag him down, the firmer his resolve became. Living among some of the worst criminal elements in the country, while knowing that he was innocent of the charges, proved to be even a greater mental obstacle to overcome. Yet he managed to stiffen his resistance to the temptation to give up on life, for he knew in his heart that even with all the negatives stacked up against him, one day he would be free and reunited with the ones he loved.

Stateville Penitentiary was a vicious, lawless unruly institution until it reached its tenth birthday in 1935. At that time, the new warden, Joseph E. Ragen, was installed by Governor Henry Horner. Under Warden Ragen, its guiding light for thirty years, Stateville achieved a reputation as a disciplined, rehabilitating penal institution without peer.

Religion was another important element in Philip's life. He and the other Jewish prisoners, most of whom had come from his neighborhood on the West Side, attended prayer services and holiday observances on a very limited basis. These were administered by visiting rabbis and the prison chaplain. Jewish mobsters, once a rarity, had become semi-prominent in criminal life, thanks to prohibition, easy money and the loose adherence to the law by the very people who were entrusted to enforce them. The twenties gave birth to the criminal element in every nationality that emigrated to these shores.

CHAPTER EIGHTEEN

Having raised the necessary funds, Jack and Rose went off in search of a capable and prestigious attorney who could work with a full and independent vigor to seek freedom for Philip and Morris. Unshackled from the Checker Taxi Company and its president Mike Sokol, the new attorney, Edgar J. Cook, proceeded to file new Petitions for Pardon over the names of Bella Fox and Rose Stuben. The Petitions for Pardon although addressed to "his Excellency, Len Small," Governor of the State of Illinois, traveled a circuitous route.

The process for filing a Petition for Pardon follows the same course now as it did then. First a petition is submitted to the Supervisor of Pardons and Paroles and then is scheduled for a hearing by the full board. After the completion of the hearing, the final recommendation goes to the governor for his action and disposition. Once the schedule is made, according to practice rather than by law, all parties of interest whether pro or con are notified. They can either submit a written protest or recommendation, or appear before the pardon board. The board conducts two distinct types of hearings. A *parole* hearing is to listen to reasons why a prisoner should be released from the remainder of his sentence. These reasons can be categorized as: good behavior in prison, rehabilitated to join society again, or of such nature that he will become a useful and productive citizen. These reasons all fall under the umbrella of being guilty of the crime committed and having paid his debt to society.

A *pardon* hearing has an entirely different connotation. It is a direct petition to redress an injustice to a prisoner who feels he has been falsely incarcerated, and would like the pardon board to re-examine the evidence and circumstances surrounding his arrest and conviction. With a pardon hearing, the prisoner's ultimate hope is total exoneration, freedom and full restoration of his/her citizenship and rights under the law.

In the Petition for Pardon, which was received June 10, 1927, Attorney Cook enumerated the most glaring points of inaccuracy and lack of conclusive evidence in the case against Philip Fox:

1.   While this touring car was passing the cab stand, several hands holding revolvers were seen to be protruding from behind the curtains. A number of shots came from the car, one of which struck the deceased and resulted in his death. None of the drivers of the Yellow Cab Company who was present was able to see any of the persons in the car, nor was able to identify the dark touring car, and none gave any evidence at all which would tend to connect any person whatsoever with the shooting;

2.   Robert Stamm, the witness who furnished the strongest portion of the circumstantial evidence against Fox, was himself under indictment in the Criminal Court of Cook County, and subsequently pleaded guilty to two counts of manslaughter, and he was represented by John F. Tyrell, a lawyer who was then associated with Attorney George F. Barrett, former Judge of the Circuit Court, who supervised the unlawful inquisition at which Morris Stuben, who was jointly tried with Philip Fox and convicted, was compelled to confess that he committed the crime charged against him. The forced confession of Stuben and the circumstantial evidence in the case seemed to put Fox in the company of Stuben and brought about Fox's conviction;

3.   In a separate trial on December 10, 1923–prior to the conviction of Fox–James Mogley, Charles Goldstein and Max Podolsky, who were named in the same indictment, charged with the same murder and tried with the same circumstantial evidence, were released when Assistant State's Attorney William A. Rittenhouse (who was the same person who prosecuted Fox and Stuben) entered a *nolle prosequi* motion, because in the opinion of Prosecutor Rittenhouse, the circumstantial evidence was insufficient to secure a conviction.

4.   The decision by the majority of the Illinois Supreme Court, in accepting the involuntary confession of Stuben, did not follow the generally accepted doctrine of the members of the Bar. They hold that an involuntary confession should be excluded from the evidence regardless of whether it is true or false on the ground that it was involuntary, and is therefore presumed to be false.

5.   Acting on the advice of his former attorney, Fox did not testify or produce any evidence at the trial before the jury. Fox

was prepared to testify in his own defense and to truthfully state facts showing that he had no participation whatever in the crime, but acting upon the advice of attorney Ahern, refrained from testifying in his own behalf. Fox was further assured that the court had committed reversible errors in not excluding the confession, and that a judgment of conviction would be reversed and the case remanded for a new trial, at which time Fox could testify to the true facts in the case.

In addition to other legal references and conclusions, Attorney Cook closed his Petition for Pardon with this final sentence: "Wherefore, your petitioner respectfully prays, the premises being considered, that your Excellency will in the exercise of his great clemency, grant the prayer of your petitioner and pardon the said Philip Fox, of the crime of which he stands convicted, and a release from said imprisonment and restoration to the right of citizenship."

Moving very slowly, as the wheels of justice usually turn, a period of one year elapsed before the Pardon and Parole Board acknowledged receipt of the petition. Time is also the chronic enemy of the prisoner and Philip was finding it more and more difficult to battle this unseen adversary, and at the same time to conquer the fear of a negative decision on the part of the Board. Violence was still erupting all about him, as the change of wardens and prison personnel did little to change the basic underlying causes of the constant prisoner rebellion. Idleness was one of the devil's tools that fed into the prison unrest.

Bella, at home during this same period, shared her husband's frustration of waiting, and also feared the possible negative ruling that might be issued by the Board. Their two children, Edward and Esther, were getting older and a little more mischievous. Edward was completing the "terrible twos" and Esther was just beginning to talk. Problems unique to children were flourishing at the Turner Avenue. residence. Scratches, scrapes and a few stitches were everyday occurrences, while childhood diseases, today easily combated, were of grave concern to worried parents back then. When one child was sick the entire population of the building worried in unison. The days grew longer and the nights more unbearable as 1927 crawled through the seasons.

CHAPTER NINETEEN

July 10, 1928, was an auspicious day in the lives of Philip Fox and Morris Stuben. It was the second significant day in their young lives and altered the course of their future. It had finally come to pass, the day of the Pardon Board hearing. The hearing was convened and called to order by its chairman, John Clabaugh. Nine other members were also present. The hearing was held at the Pardon and Parole Board headquarters in Springfield, Illinois.

It was a sweltering July day, and the clatter of the new-fangled electric fans did little to harmonize with the mixture of outside noises entering the open windows. Open shirt collars and rolled-up sleeves were the dress code of this day.

Upon learning that the matter before them concerned the Checker Cab Company, Chairman Clabaugh immediately excused himself from voting on any final decisions in this matter. As he explained, some two years before he was appointed to the Pardon Board, he was approached several times by Checker Cab to represent them in certain matters for which he was offered a rather large sum of money for a five year period. Even though he declined the offer and had no connection with them, he still felt that it would give the appearance of impropriety if he were to participate in this case. Though he knew it was a display of supersensitiveness on his part, he did not want anyone to have the opportunity to say he showed favoritism for one side or the other.

Former Judge C.H. Jenkins from Springfield, who now represented Philip and Morris, opened the proceedings with this introductory explanation.

"I appreciate that this is a very hot day, and will undertake in my presentation to be as brief as possible. If the Board please this is a conviction which grew out of and is part and parcel of a purely Chicago situation, wherein two rival cab companies, namely the Checker Cab Company and the Yellow Cab Company had business differences in the field of transportation, in the city of Chicago.

"As a result of these differences, and their undertaking by themselves to adjust their differences violence ensued, violence indulged in by the employees of both companies. This violence finally resulted in the killing of an employee of the Yellow Cab Co.

"It was deemed necessary, apparently, by the officials and legal advisors of the opposing cab company that somebody be convicted, and that an example be made. Accordingly Fox and Stuben, together with several others, three finally being indicted besides Fox and Stuben for the killing of the Yellow Cab driver on the date set forth on the petition.

"Fox and Stuben were arrested on suspicion without warrant and were taken to the State's Attorney's office. I do not mean to criticize the attorney who defended Fox and Stuben at their trial, but he led them to believe that the trial court in the admission of confessions which had been made by Fox and Stuben, had committed error, and that when the matter finally came to the Supreme Court, the case would be reversed and remanded for a new trial. Therefore Fox and Stuben on advice of counsel, were not permitted to take the stand in their defense, so that the record rests upon the uncontradicted testimony of the witnesses offered by the people together with the confession of Stuben, the confession of Fox being denied by the court.

"I feel no hesitancy in saying to this Board that Fox and Stuben are no more guilty of the commission of the crime for which they stand convicted, than are probably fifteen hundred other cab drivers, employed by the Checker Cab Co.

"It is evident that from a reading of the opinion, both of the majority of the Supreme Court and by the dissenting opinion filed by Judge Duncan, that Fox and Stuben were selected as the victims to stand as a sacrifice for all of the trouble and all the violence and all of the illegal things that had been done by the employees of the Checker Cab Company in this cab war, each seeking a monopoly upon the streets of Chicago."

Following his opening statements, Attorney Jenkins proceeded to lay out the facts and fallacies of the case. His dissertation led the members of the Pardon Board through the prejudicial interest of the witness against Fox and Stuben, and the obvious distortions of the truth. The entire litany of violence perpetrated on Fox and Stuben to extricate their confessions was again stated for the Board.

Judge Thompson's majority opinion and Judge Duncan's minority opinion of the Illinois Supreme Court were recited, nearly in their entirety, to focus on the errors of the Trial Court, and the defense attorneys. The Pardon Board listened with disbelief to the fact that the interrogator in the State's Attorney's office was Attorney Barrett, who had no official capacity, but, on the contrary, was the chief legal officer of the Yellow Cab Company. Attorney Jenkins at this point in his recitation painted a very obvious conclusion pertaining to the confessions.

Those parties and officials who were interested in securing a conviction decided that the three other defendants originally indicted with Fox and Stuben were hardened characters, not employed as cab drivers, and would not succumb to the severe punishment about to be administered in the State's Attorney's office in order to obtain a confession. The three were released in a separate trial at a later date for lack of evidence. Fox and Stuben both being younger, and never in trouble with the law before this incident, and both being working stiffs, were chosen as the two most vulnerable candidates to crack under the relentless pressure. The confessions were considered of utmost importance in this trial as there were not any eyewitnesses to the killing.

Attorney Jenkins, in his ongoing presentation to the Pardon Board, relied heavily on the minority opinion of the learned Judge John Duncan of the Illinois Supreme Court. Judge Duncan's outrage at the manner in which the confessions were obtained, and along with the glaring trial errors, began to weigh heavily on the decision making process of the Board.

Summing up the initial offering of facts, Attorney Jenkins concluded with this appeal: "This incident occurred seven years ago. Since that time the differences between the cab companies, are at least, at a truce and there is no warfare. The conditions existing between the two companies are reasonably pleasant. Fox and Stuben have served in the Stateville Penitentiary at Joliet for two and one half years. They have been subjected to all the ignominies of two trials.

They were beaten severely, and about everything that could be done to a human being has been done to them, and I say to you they were not guilty. It is time that they be permitted to go out of the penitentiary, and go back to their families. They have paid the necessary price and have done in the way of a sacrifice all that might be desired by the Yellow Cab Company and by Society. They are in there after the cab war is over and this is an appeal, gentlemen of the Board, let them go back and believe they are properly entitled to their liberty. I thank you."

Members of the Board who sat through the opening statements by Attorney Jenkins were now ready to ask questions:

MR. CANNON: This killing happened in 1921?

MR. JENKINS: Yes, sir, and I think they went to the penitentiary in January of 1926.

MR. SAWYER: What was the necessity for the delay in the trial?

MR. JENKINS: There were two trials.

MR. SAWYER: Why did it take two or three years to try the case?

MR. JENKINS: I don't know.

MR. CANNON: They were placed on trial April 1922, and in June of 1925 they were tried the second time. Was this merely a general fight?

MR. JENKINS: It was the result of general trouble. I might have analyzed the evidence more. Some witnesses testified having seen Fox and Stuben in a pool room on the night of the murder; naturally this pool room being a Checker Cab station, they would have been there, but there is not a thing except the circumstances of being there which testified to by persons who, on cross examinations showed their interests to the Checker Cab Co. or the Yellow Cab Co. and but for the effect of the illegal confession, there was not a thing to hang a verdict on.

MR. CANNON: The chief witness is now in Joliet?

MR. JENKINS: Yes, I think doing fourteen years for murder. His name is Stamm.

MR. RHOADES: Your contention is that Fox and Stuben were convicted on the confession of Stuben?

MR. JENKINS: Yes, sir.

MR. RHOADES: Did he later repudiate his confession?

MR. JENKINS: They were not given an opportunity on the advice of their attorneys, they were not permitted to take the stand, counsel believing the court committed such errors, that they would be entitled to a new trial. In this advice their counsel was wrong. Throughout both the majority and dissenting opinions filed by the Supreme Court, it is clear had it not been for the confession extorted from Stuben, there would have been no conviction.

At this point in the hearings, Mr. Benjamin Samuels, attorney for the Yellow Cab Company and soon to become president of Yellow Cab Company of Chicago, interjected on behalf of Yellow Cab. He immediately denied the existence of any cab warfare at the time of the killing, although the Chicago newspapers carried this headline story for weeks. He tried to paint a picture of everyday normal business intercourse between the two companies.

In spite of his own admission that there were no eyewitnesses, he tried to convince the Board of the guilt of Fox and Stuben, by again extolling the deceitful and prejudicial testimony of the rewarded witnesses. Mr. Samuels also stated that he was present at the interrogation of Fox and Stuben, and that he did not witness any abuse or violence perpetrated upon the persons of Fox and Stuben, despite the physical evidence to the contrary. In fact, Mr. Samuels was even bold enough to suggest that the three prominent physicians who examined Fox and Stuben were bought and paid for their description of the results of the beatings.

MR. JENSEN: How did Fox get the lump on his head?

MR. SAMUELS: There are a lot of ways to get that by paying a little money to a good doctor.

MR. JENSEN: You stated Fox and Stuben testified before the Grand Jury as to their part in the crime. How do you know that? Is not the Grand Jury hearings supposed to remain secret?

MR. SAMUELS: Only the facts of the State's Attorney's record and the minutes I saw.

MR. JENSEN: The Grand jury action is not open to anyone, is it?

MR. SAMUELS: Yes, in the trial of Fox and Stuben's murder case I saw all the records and the stenographic transcript. I was interested on behalf of the State.

MR. JENSEN: Did you help in the prosecution?

MR. SAMUELS: I did not.

MR. LaROCHELLE: (Assistant State's Attorney) After a person testifies before the Grand Jury they come out and make a statement to two reporters in the adjoining room and they are asked to repeat substantially the same story they told before the Grand Jury, and it is made part of the files.

MR. RHOADES: Is that accessible to anybody who wants to see it?

MR. LaROCHELLE: Any assistant State's Attorney or anybody in the prosecution of the case.

Mr. Samuels' partisanship became more and more apparent as the hearing went on. Mr. Samuels, who was not involved in the prosecution of the case, apparently had illegal access to the transcript of the Grand Jury, and was willing to use them to keep Fox and Stuben incarcerated in Stateville for the full length of their life terms. Despite his alleged great knowledge of the law, he tried to obfuscate the difference in the law between a parole and a pardon. He tried strenuously to convince the Board that they were violating the parole rule, when this particular hearing was a pardon hearing. Under Illinois law in 1928, a person convicted of a capital crime could not have a parole hearing until twenty years after his or her conviction. The purpose of a pardon hearing was to investigate new evidence and testimony to establish the innocence of a person falsely convicted, and to adjudicate the matter as quickly as possible.

MR. SAMUELS: It seems almost audacious for a man after serving two years of a life sentence when the parole law says they cannot ask for a *parole* until twenty years after conviction, and I say it is absolutely audacious to expect a pardon board in the face of the stringent law for parole. It is no fault of ours that the other three are not convicted.

MR. RHOADES: Why weren't they convicted?

MR. SAMUELS: The State's Attorney said he did not want to proceed. He would not go ahead. He said he did not think he had enough to convict.

MR. CANNON: The Supreme Court referred to Samuel Miller, one of the chief witnesses, who had at the time of the offense been employed by the Paulina Street station of the Checker Taxi Company. On cross-examination Miller admitted that he left the employ of the Checker Taxi Company in September 1921, and that he had since been employed as an investigator by the Yellow Cab Co. That the first time he revealed the information he had regarding the ownership of the guns and the conversations he had with Fox and Stuben was after he had trouble with the Checker Taxi Company and left its employ, and thereafter he went to an officer of the Yellow Cab Co., rather than the Police or State's Attorney, and gave him the information about the guns and the statements.

MR. SAMUELS: That is true, I am not belittling that at all, but may I inject one thing?

MR. CANNON: (Reading from the Supreme Court decision) "Stamm stated on cross-examination that the first time he told the story about seeing the five persons indicted leave in an automobile with the declaration they were going to kill Yellow Cab drivers was when Miller came to see him about the matter after the jury failed to agree at the first trial."

MR. SAMUELS: That is correct. I am not questioning that.

MR. CANNON: Have these two gentlemen any previous record?

MR. LaROCHELLE: I don't know. I don't think so.

MR. CHAIRMAN: You make the statement there was a touring car passing that particular place where this man was killed, and shots fired from that touring car, containing five people. Stuben and Fox were tried. The jury in the first trial wanted to hang them.

There were three other men in the car and their cases were dropped for lack of evidence.

MR. LaROCHELLE: That was three years later.

MR. RHOADES: I cannot reconcile myself to that fact, that the jury wanted to hang two of them, while the other three went free for lack of evidence.

When the following question was asked by Mr. Benson of the Board, "Are the same officers in charge of the Checker Taxi Cab Company now as were in charge of the Checker Taxi Cab Company then," the answer given by Samuels, "No sir, not one," is rather confusing and does much to cloud his motives. He had been involved with the Yellow Cab Company and Mr. John Hertz since before the cab wars started, and knew for a certainty that Michael Sokol was president and chief executive officer of Checker Cab Company long before the murder of Skirven in 1921. Sokol continued in that position uninterrupted until his death in the 1960s.

MR. BENSON: Did the postmortem reveal the caliber of the bullet?

MR. LaROCHELLE: I think it was a thirty-eight.

MR. BENSON: And Fox had a thirty-two?

MR. LaROCHELLE: I think so.

MR. BENSON: What kind did Stuben have?

MR. LaROCHELLE: Stuben drove the car.

MR. JENSEN: What was the caliber of the other guns?

MR. LaROCHELLE: There were five guns mixed up at Brown's Pool Room.

MR. BENSON: Which one of the guns killed the man?

MR. SAMUELS: I think the record will show it was a thirty-eight.

MR. BENSON: And Fox had a thirty-two. According to the record, Fox's gun had not been fired.

MR. SAMUELS: Fox admitted he fired four shots.

MR. BENSON: I cannot find it.

MR. JENKINS: That is not in the record.

MR. CHAIRMAN: Is the confession part of the record?

MR. JENKINS: No, it is not.

MR. SAMUELS: The confession is not there. The other man had testified there were five or six shots fired from the men in the back of the car.

MR. BENSON: We cannot take into consideration a statement not in the record.

MR. BENSON: According to the record it was a thirty-eight bullet that killed this man?

MR. SAMUELS: That is true, and this man Fox had a thirty-two.

MR. BENSON: It evidently was one of the others who were not prosecuted who fired the shot.

MR. SAMUELS: Your conclusion is absolutely correct, there is no getting away from it.

MR. BENSON: They were not prosecuted.

Once again the mystery of the three men who were not prosecuted surfaced to the attention of the Board. Who employed them? Who paid them? What was their connection to the cab company? These questions remain as unsolvable today as they were back then. One can only surmise that their entire job description consisted of muscle and mayhem.

MR. BENSON: Were the three men who were not prosecuted, employees of the Checker Cab Co.?

A VOICE: They were not on the payroll of the Checker Co.

MR. LaROCHELLE: Were they employed by the Union?

A VOICE: They were supposed to be employed by the union.

MR. CANNON: Were they or were they not on the payroll of the taxi company?

MR. SAMUELS: I say they were. I want to say however in fairness to the present officials of the Checker Cab Co., at the time this took place, I don't think any of them were officials of the company, or the association.

CHAIRMAN: You are attorney for the Checker Cab Company are you not?

A VOICE: Yes sir.

THE CHAIRMAN: There is one observation the chairman would like to make regarding the parole law and conviction of this case by a jury or a court. Keep in mind, in matters of pardon, the Governor's authority is not only supreme, but he has the right to revoke any parole or pardon or anything else. And even though there have been jury convictions, there have been cases which would been in place so as to advise the Governor, that he may act to correct them. There would be no remedy for any person. Courts and juries make have been horrible miscarriages of justice, if the machinery had not mistakes the same as parole Boards and others. There comes a time when it is the duty of this Board to examine the conduct of the trial, evidence and all of the facts having any part whatsoever in the conviction of these men for the purpose of determining whether the Governor would be justified in correcting an injustice, exercising clemency, mercy or whatnot. This is not a court of review. We sit necessary as a court of investigation as to what is the proper thing to do.

CHAIRMAN: Justice comes ahead of mercy.

MR JENKINS: The Constitution was totally disregarded in this case. The men who assaulted Fox and Stuben were guilty not only of assault and battery, but assault with intent to kill because they would have killed Fox and Stuben unless they made the confessions these men asked for and wanted.

The remark or observation has been made that this is a court of mercy. If the honorable Board please, Fox and Stuben are not appearing here asking for mercy. They are asking for justice. They are asking to be given that consideration which they should have had when their case was before the court, and which, had the Supreme Court followed the uniform long line of decisions that existed for more than seventy-five years before that. If the Supreme Court had followed that line and found error in the practice on account of improper admission of the confession made by Stuben, the case

-89-

would have been remanded for a new trial, they then would have taken the stand and been acquitted.

CHAIRMAN: Any further questions? If not we will call the next case.

Thus ended the Pardon Board hearing, the final hurdle to freedom in the Illinois judicial system. It was waiting time once again. The Pardon Board recommendation, and the action taken by the Governor would be the last act in this fight for justice.

CHAPTER TWENTY

Bella's hopes and those of the Fox family began to escalate. Attorney Jenkins' presentation before the Board was well received, and the pointed questions by various members of the Board seemed to give small indications that they believed that Fox and Stuben were mistreated and that circumstantial evidence against them was weak at best. Her stoic countenance to the contrary, Bella's heart beat a little faster during the balance of that summer of 1928, with the thought that her beloved husband might soon be released and they would be reunited as a normal family.

Prison routine had not changed for Philip, but the flicker of hope was again burning a little brighter now that the Board had given his case a thorough airing. He was convinced from the beginning of the first trial that if he ever could present all the true facts in the case, the outcome would be a favorable one. His conduct in prison up to this time had been one of a model prisoner, except for two separate incidents. In June of 1926, he was accused of being "insolent" and put in "solitary confinement;" and in March of 1927, he was charged with "talking in line" and again the punishment was "solitary confinement."

It was considered a minor miracle to serve almost three years at Stateville during this unruly and undisciplined period, and only have incurred two minor infractions on one's record. Inmates were still running the cell blocks with intimidation and violence. Guards were as brutal and corrupt as ever.

The pall that continued to hang over the family had been lifted for a time by the special events in the lives of Philip's two younger sisters. Bertha had met Morris Hyman, a young linotype operator who was working for the *Jewish Daily Forward*. This was a vital publication for the Yiddish-speaking immigrant population, as it had an advice column that disseminated important information on how to get along in the United States. They fell in love and were married in May of 1927. Rose had completed her studies at a business college and was now employed by a Chicago law firm specializing in real estate law.

Max and Marion and all of Philip's siblings were eagerly awaiting the recommendation of the Pardon Board. Rose, along with her brother Jack, continued to work tirelessly toward the goal of getting their brother released from prison. They rallied the drivers, raised more funds, and conferred with the attorneys on a daily basis. They too had their spirits lifted, as they had accomplished the first half of their goal, which was the hearing of the case before the Pardon Board. Their only action now was to await the recommendation of the Board. They would not know if they had achieved total success for another six months.

The waning months of 1928 saw a mixed bag of economic positions. The majority of the population was still enjoying growth and prosperity. Other segments of the populace found themselves in dire straits; the farmers, miners and mill workers continued in a downward spiral, while the country in the past decade had produced more millionaires than ever before. The market continued its upward movement with no indication that it would ever decline.

Fox's Bakery on Ogden Avenue was doing well in this middle period of the 1920s, but the hard work associated with this business had not subsided for Marion and Max. On top of her normal duties divided between the bakery and home, she added the continuous visitations of every second Tuesday to her oldest son in Stateville prison. Her family was growing larger and the need for her emotional support and common sense approach to life grew proportionately.

Due to improper ventilation and the very nature of the bakery industry, Max was developing a deep cough. Long hours and flour dust inhalation were beginning to take their toll on his physical well-being. However, he never deviated from his well-known integrity and deep religious beliefs. His business philosophy was simple: turn out a top quality product and sell it at a reasonable price. He was charitable to a fault. In addition to his constant donations to Jewish relief organizations and various synagogues in the West Side area, he maintained a constant charitable policy in his business establishment as well. Each Friday at noon he would close the store for business, but would keep the doors open and give away to the poor all the remaining unsold merchandise so that they also would have food to prepare for the Sabbath. By Friday noon he would bank the fires in the wood-burning ovens, and allow the people to cook their Saturday meal, known as a "cholent," a combination stew of vegetables, beans, meat and fruit, slow-cooked for twenty-four hours. It was one of the traditional foods of the European *shtetlach* (little towns in Eastern Europe).

Rosh Hashana (the Jewish New Year), Yom Kippur (the Day of Atonement), and Sukkos (the festival of Tabernacles) seemed a little brighter this holiday season of 1928, for they knew the Governor must soon make his decision, as the term of his office was coming to an end.

CHAPTER TWENTY-ONE

With Chairman Clabaugh conducting the meeting, the Board began its deliberations. They had requested and received all pertinent documents and information from various sources germane to this Petition. Letters from the State's Attorney, trial judge and opponents were also received, each voicing his opinion, or neutral position, as in the case of Judge Gemmill. The Board digested all this material, and was now ready to issue its recommendation to Governor Len Small.

The summation and recommendation read as follows: "The crime for which Fox and Stuben were sentenced to Joliet Prison grew out of the wars between the Yellow and Checker Cab Companies of Chicago. Fox and Stuben were convicted on circumstantial evidence. Three associates who were indicted with them, were not convicted. Their cases were nollied by the State's Attorney. This case was appealed to the Supreme Court. A dissenting opinion was filed by Judge Duncan which stated that Fox and Stuben were selected as the victims to stand as a sacrifice for all of the trouble between the two cab companies.

"At the July 1928 term of the Parole Board, sitting as a Pardon Board, Mr. Benjamin Samuels of the Yellow Cab Co. appeared in protest. He admitted that Fox and Stuben were convicted on circumstantial evidence and they had never been positively identified as the men who fired the shot. The entire record indicates that duress and violence were used to secure testimony against these men. In the first trial the jury disagreed. The judge did not permit the confessions to be used inasmuch as one was received by violence and fear and third degree methods. In the second trial the confession made by Stuben was permitted to be used.

"Assistant State's Attorney LaRochelle represented the State's Attorney's office at the hearing held in Springfield in July. Both Mr. Samuels and Mr. LaRochelle admitted that there was no positive evidence that Fox and Stuben had anything to do with the killing."

"In view of the statements made we are of the opinion that both Morris Stuben and Philip Fox have served sufficient time for whatever part they may have taken in the taxicab war and feel that this is a case in which the Governor may properly exercise his pardoning power.

"Recommendation

"We, therefore, recommend that the prayer of the petition be granted; that the sentences of Philip Fox and Morris Stuben be commuted to expire at once."

The recommendation was approved and signed by the entire Board, and forwarded to the Governor's office. On December 21, 1928, the recommendation was approved and signed by the Director of Prisons, and then received the final signature of the Governor of the State of Illinois, Len Small. It was official.

Philip Fox and Morris Stuben were free men. The miracle that Philip and Bella and the entire Fox family had hoped for, prayed for and worked so hard for at last had come true. Philip and Morris were released late in the afternoon of December 21, 1928. They were on their way home to Chicago after serving three years in the maximum security prison at the Stateville Penitentiary for a murder they did not commit.

Irony and destiny at certain points in one's life seem to have an affinity for interconnecting. The irony of the situation in Philip's life became apparent on the morning of December 22, 1928, when the Chicago dailies carried the story of the Governor's action pardoning three killers, two union executives, a cab manufacturer, and two lifers, Philip Fox and Morris Stuben.

The headline article of the *Chicago Daily Tribune* led with the following paragraph: "Five convicted murderers, two of them once under the death sentence, were given Christmas presents in the form of immediate commutation of sentence or complete pardons yesterday by Governor Small. The executive action was announced after a meeting of Governor Small, with the members of the state board of pardons and paroles at Kankakee, Illinois."

The ironic connection to Philip, however, was the story of the cab manufacturer. According to the article in the *Chicago Daily News*, dated December 22, 1928, "Morris Markin, the former cab manufacturer, pardoned yesterday, was found guilty four years ago of violating the blue sky law, and sentenced to spend thirty days in

GIVES PARDON TO POTZ, ONCE DOOMED TO DIE

Dec 22 1928

Four Other Slayers Escape Penalties.

(Picture on back page.)

Five convicted murderers, two of them once under death sentences, were given Christmas presents in the form of immediate commutations of sentence or complete pardons yesterday by Gov. Small. The executive action was announced after a meeting of Gov. Small with the members of the state board of pardons and paroles at Kankakee, the governor's home. It was reported that other cases were under consideration.

Chicago Tribune, **December 22, 1928**

96

The principal beneficiary of the first batch of pardons or commutations to be issued by the governor before he leaves office, probably on Jan. 14, was Ignatz Potz, thrice the recipient of executive clemency. He was sentenced to death in 1922 for the murder of William Peterson, a motorcycle policeman of Winthrop Harbor, Ill.

Sam Washington, a Negro, was the other man, once in the shadow of the gallows, to be relieved of his sentence, which was first commuted to life imprisonment. He was convicted of slaying Minnie Moore, his common law wife, in 1925. This commutation is said to be the result of the direct intervention of Hinton G. Clabaugh, chairman of the parole board.

Taxi Killers Are Freed.

Washington, like Potz, was literally snatched from the gallows at the last minute. He claimed that the killing was an accident.

Phillip Fox and Morris Steuben, who were sentenced to life terms for the murder of Thomas Skirven, a Yellow taxicab chauffeur, during the taxicab war in 1921, were also given immediate commutations. They were convicted and sentenced after two bitterly fought trials, and later appealed their convictions to the Supreme court. They have been serving not more than two years.

Chicago Tribune, **December 22, 1928 (cont.)**

97

FREES SHIELDS, KANE AND WALSH

Chicago Daily News
Dec 22-1928

Morris Markin, ex-Head of Checker Cab, Also 'Out'; Is Fugitive.

FIVE KILLERS RELEASED

Hard on the heels of the pardoning of five convicted killers, Gov. Small today granted commutations to three labor leaders and a former president of the Checker Cab Manufacturing company.

A messenger, carrying an executive Christmas present arrived at the county jail with pardons freeing forthwith Roy ("Muckles") Shields, former business agent of the painters' union, and Patrick Kane, former business agent for the plumbers' union. The men were serving a one-year sentence in the county jail imposed six years ago when a jury found them guilty of conspiracy to extort money from building contractors.

Thomas Walsh, former business agent of the sheet-metal workers' union, who was convicted with them, will be freed March 18. The men disappeared when they lost their fight in the Supreme court and did not begin serving their sentence un-

Phillip Fox and Morris Steuben, sentenced to life terms for the murder of Thomas Skirven, a taxicab chauffeur, in 1921, and Paul Lindsey, who four years ago began serving a fourteen-year sentence for the killing of a gasoline station owner, are the others who will be permitted to spend Christmas outside of the prison as a result of the governor's action.

Potz three times has been given official clemency. Only a few hours before he was to have been hanged on June 16, 1922, the governor extended him a sixty-day stay of execution and later commuted his sentence to life imprisonment.

This stay came while the governor himself was on trial at Waukegan on a charge of withholding public funds while state treasurer, and he said it was granted because of a death bed request of Mrs. Small.

union, who was sentenced with [illegible] will be freed March 18. The men disappeared when they lost their fight in the Supreme court and did not begin serving their sentence until this year, Shields on April 20; Kane, May 9, and Walsh, Sept. 19.

Stock Operator Freed

Morris Markin, the former cab manufacturer, pardoned, was found guilty four years ago of violating the blue sky law and sentenced to spend thirty days in the county jail, has never been apprehended so will never have to serve a day of his sentence.

Ignatz Potz, sentenced to death in 1922 for the murder of Motorcycle Policeman William Peterson of Winthrop Harbor, Ill., who twice before had been extended executive clemency by the governor, was one of the five murderers released.

Sam Washington, colored, who also stood in the shadow of the gallows until his sentence was changed to life imprisonment for the killing of Minnie Moore, his common-law wife in Chicago, was another.

Fox and Morris Stuben be commuted to expire at once.

APPROVED:

_____
DIRECTOR

APPROVED:

_____
GOVERNOR

DATE: _December 21-1928_

CHAIRMAN
_____
MEMBER
_____
MEMBER
_____
MEMBER
_____
MEMBER
_____
MEMBER
_____
MEMBER
_____
MEMBER
_____
MEMBER

Signature page of recommendation of State of Illinois Parol Board, sitting as a pardon board, recommending the commutation of the sentences of Philip Fox and Morris Stuben, with the signature of Governor Small approving the recommendation.

county jail plus a fine of $5,000.00. He has never been apprehended, so he will never have to serve a day of his sentence."

The violation of the "Blue Sky Law" under Illinois statutes pertains to the illegal or fraudulent trading, selling or manipulation of securities, stocks and bonds. Back in 1926, John Hertz, Yellow Cab Company's owner and founder, had slowly begun to fade from the cab industry. With the star of John Hertz descending in the taxi industry, another star was rising in the person of Morris Markin, who was to become an even brighter light in the field of transportation.

Morris Markin arrived in the United States in the middle of World War I as a young tailor, who in his native Russia worked as a supervisor in a clothing manufacturing plant. With the dual blessings of luck and business acumen, in the next few years Markin had accumulated a large sum of money manufacturing pants for the United States Army. Combining his money and financial skills, Markin was able to purchase several defunct companies in the automotive industry which planted him squarely in the transportation field with his creation of the Checker Taxi Manufacturing Company. By 1926, he found himself amongst the big boys in manufacturing cabs. General Motors, Yellow Cab Manufacturing, Dodge Bros., Paramount and DeSoto were some of his larger competitors in this new field. His company's designs and ideas set the standards for cabs in the United States. Fueled by his drive to succeed in what almost overnight became a highly competitive industry, Markin realized that he had to create his own market and niche, where the demand for his cabs would continue to grow. He concluded wisely that the place to sell cabs was to his own cab companies. With this incentive, Markin started buying taxi transportation companies.

After his conviction in 1924, Markin removed himself from the presidency of Checker Taxi Manufacturing, installed an assistant in that position, and then left the state to avoid serving the thirty day sentence. He did not return to take back the official control of the Checker Taxi Manufacturing until his pardon in late 1928. In 1929, Markin acquired the Chicago Yellow Cab Company, and just a few years later bought the Checker Taxi Company. He would become Philip's ultimate boss. Through purchases and acquisitions, Morris

Markin eventually became the largest single owner of taxi cabs in the world. He would also hold the distinction in years to come of owning the only cab manufacturing facility in the United States.[2]

---

[2] Gorman Gilbert and Robert E. Samuels, *The Taxicab* (Chappel Hill, N.C., and London: The University of North Carolina Press, 1982) 38-73.

CHAPTER TWENTY-TWO

It was a mixture of pandemonium and jubilation that filled the air at dusk on that day, as Philip ascended the staircase to his apartment. Waiting at the top of the stairs was a welcoming committee of the screaming and crying women in his life. His mother was gasping for breath as she hugged her eldest son tightly to her breast. Bella's face was streaked with tears as she awaited her turn to express the deep emotions and love she was feeling at this moment. Philip's sisters alternately took turns, slapping him on the back and stroking his face, competing with their tears to express their joy. The children of the building and the closest neighbors, having heard the commotion, rushed to the hallway, only adding to the tumult of this boisterous homecoming scene.

No stranger, or even an unrelated observer, could possibly comprehend the depth of despair, concern and humiliation this family had been feeling since the arrest of Philip back on June 10th, 1921. It went beyond Max and Marion and their children. The feelings reached into the extended family of Marion, both in Chicagoland and South Bend, Indiana.

The next day the official homecoming celebration kicked into high gear. A large banner was placed across the balcony front of the upper floor apartment of the building. Relatives and friends were streaming in from all over the Midwest. Warm greetings and expressions of relief and joy abounded in this atmosphere of a "new beginning."

Freedom and the restoration of his citizenship, with all of its rights and privileges, was an exhilarating feeling that first week following his release. He renewed his marital relationship with his wife, Bella, and began building his paternal bond with his two young children. Other family members and his loyal friends arrived daily to express their joy at his release. Their show of faith in his innocence never diminished. It was the "Chanukah" season, and the Jewish holiday known as both the "Festival of Freedom" and the "Festival of Lights" took on an additional dimension of celebration.

Reality of a normal life became apparent once again and Philip knew he must find employment to support his family. Being reluctant to return to the taxi industry at first, he also realized the difficulties he would encounter in applying for other positions. Answering the question of where he was employed the last three years would be the main obstacle. After due deliberation, and the necessity of a weekly paycheck, Philip allowed himself to be convinced by Mike Sokol to return to Checker, not as a driver, but rather as a journeyman plumber to maintain and repair all of the various facilities within the company.

Chicago, at the conclusion of each year, brings out for display its finest adornments and sparkling glitter during the Thanksgiving, Christmas and New Year's holiday season. Combined with the glistening white snow and brightly colored lights, Chicago's otherwise drab shopping thoroughfares become alive with sound and color and good cheer. This holiday season of 1928 was no different, except for the fact that this would be the last robust holiday shopping season for the next decade.

On January second, nineteen hundred and twenty-nine, normal life started anew for Philip, as he once again began the daily routine of earning a living. It was not long before the company realized that they needed Philip's executive abilities and leadership qualities, for the drivers had not forgotten him. They promoted him to "Road Superintendent," a position he held for the next sixteen years. He was given a reasonable salary for the time and a car allowance, which enabled him to purchase a new car and cover automobile expenses. His duties consisted of hands-on supervision of the drivers, trying to steer them clear of trouble, while at the same time doing as much public relations work as possible.

During this same period, Al Capone and his gangsters were solidifying their position as the number one mob in Chicago. Murdered bodies were found daily as testimony to the strength and aggression of the Capone mob. The myths and legends of Al Capone were growing out of all proportion to reality. Prohibition was still in full swing and the temptation to earn additional money, albeit illegal, was too great for a large number of drivers. Philip often found himself in police stations or courthouses, trying to extricate the drivers from the misdemeanor charges and other minor infractions of the law. His efforts and fairness on their behalf were becoming more well-known, even greater than before. Drivers brought their problems with the company to him, and he acted as a mediator between them and management. He considered working outdoors another fantastic benefit of the job as he had not had that privilege over the previous three years. This benefit only added to the pleasure of the freedom he now enjoyed.

At about the same period that Philip had returned to a normal life, his youngest sister, Rose, had completed the wedding cycle of the Fox siblings. Rose had fallen in love and married a handsome young man, whose name was Maurice Halap. Maurice was a certified physical education teacher, and one of his first endeavors was to establish a fitness and health club in the famous Edgewater Beach Hotel in Chicago. They were married in a civil ceremony late in 1928 and then entered into the religious bonds in March of 1929. Philip's gratitude towards his sister Rose was unflagging, for it was she who was the inspiration and the driving force in the family's efforts to obtain his freedom.

Bella and Philip's deep love for each other and the three year separation were the primary ingredients that produced their third child, just a little over nine months after Philip's release from prison. Bella gave birth to a beautiful baby girl on September 29, 1929, and they named her Helen.

Prior to the arrival of their new baby, Philip and Bella had realized that the apartment they were sharing with Philip's parents was too small and that it was time to find a place of their own. Philip's sister Fanny and her husband Sam had recently relocated to a new apartment building just a few blocks from Turner Avenue at 18th Street and Trumbull Avenue. This new 12-flat was owned by a cousin of Sam, and at the suggestion of his sister, Bella and Philip moved to one of the new vacant apartments at that location. With the onset of the Depression, it became apparent that the portion of his salary that he had been contributing to the household on Turner Avenue would be sorely missed.

The bakery business had taken a downturn following the path of their customers' incomes. Max and Marion had extended more and more credit to the poor and non-working families to help them stave off hunger. As a result of their unselfish charity, their cash flow suffered, as most of the credit extended was never repaid.

Philip had signed a one year lease and could not move his family back, at least for the immediate future. He did, however, continue to contribute as much as he possibly could to his parents. Life alone in this new apartment promoted a more relaxed atmosphere for this young couple and their three children.

The excesses of the Nineteen-Twenties had reached its zenith in the latter part of twenty-nine. The descent from that dizzying height did not slide at a moderate pace, but cascaded down with a loud roar and a deafening crash. People who invested in the stock market and purchased stock on margin with very little money down had to pay the piper. It all began on "Black Thursday," October 24, 1929. Panic erupted at the stock exchange, as the continuous stream of sell orders poured in. Accounts purchased on margin were forced to liquidate, and this fueled the panic flames.

As fresh investment money hurried in from concerned bankers, the market stabilized some and quieted down over that weekend. By the following Tuesday, October 29, panic had set in once again, and finally, by the end of that day, it was all over. Fifteen billion dollars in market value had disappeared. It was the beginning of the end for prosperity. Unemployment had gone from seven hundred thousand to approximately three million people in one month. Thus the decade ended, not with a bang, but with a low, wailing whimper.

CHAPTER TWENTY-THREE

Despite the depression, Morris Markin was continuing his aggressive acquisitions in pursuit of his goal to own the taxi industry in Chicago. After completing his purchase of the Yellow Cab Company, by buying the remaining stock from John Hertz, and his earlier purchase of Parmelee Transportation Company, which owned a large block of Yellow Cab stock, he set his sights on the last huge remaining competitor in Chicago, the Checker Taxi Company.

It was through a double frontal assault on the independent Checker drivers that he was able to accomplish his goal. Over the years, he had sold a large number of new cabs to the Checker drivers on credit, from his Checker Taxi Manufacturing Company. Now that the Depression had set in hard, it was time to make his move. Markin began calling in his past due markers. Because of the poor economic conditions, the drivers were unable to meet their obligations, and thus forfeited their cabs and medallions to Markin for settlement. He had formed the nucleus for his takeover, and now activated the second phase of his plan.

Mike Sokol was a close friend of Markin, and had agreed with Markin's plan to unite the association into a solid taxi company under the Markin banner. Sokol, who had extended large sums of money to the drivers for the required insurance policies and maintenance costs, used the same strategy as Markin, and called in all his notes due, with the same results. Sokol then sold his interests to Markin, and he became president of the Checker Taxi Company. The other few remaining independent drivers of the association faded from activity in time through attrition. Sokol remained in charge of the day to day operations of Checker as president until his passing.

One of the residual fall-outs of the Depression was being played out on the streets of Chicago. A large number of the newly unemployed, who had not lost their cars to the creditors, decided the taxi industry was fair game. They took to the streets with a vengeance. Potential passengers were solicited in the middle of the streets, street car islands, and all intersections and walkways. The more desperate solicitors reduced their fares well below that charged by the street cars and buses, and literally decimated the revenue of the mass transit systems. Trying to keep peace and discipline among the Checker drivers in this chaotic atmosphere was another, and tougher, facet of Philip's job. Fights were erupting continually, as the machines and their operators bumped, pushed and tried to out-maneuver each other to reach the potential passenger first. Philip was caught up in an emotional dilemma during these altercations. He felt deeply for the unlicensed driver who was trying to feed his family, but at the same time he knew his loyalty lay with the company and the legal operator. He tried to settle the argument in the most amicable manner possible.

During this convulsive period in our country, passengers were often injured, but could not receive compensation for their injuries, as the greater percentage of these maverick operators did not have any insurance. As the competition increased, the fare rates went even lower, and many legitimate operators were forced into bankruptcy. Drivers once again had to turn to illegitimate means to earn money. Bootlegging, rum running, fencing and selling of stolen goods, and rolling drunken passengers were some of the illegal activities that were employed.

Unable to control this situation with their police force, the larger cities began implementing ordinances to limit the number of cabs on their streets. By enforcing these regulations, the unlicensed cabs started to disappear from the city's thoroughfares. Along with limiting the number of permits, tougher regulations were being passed in order to control the taxi and transportation industries, so that this debilitating situation could not arise again. Philip's voice was one of reason. Without him and people like him in the industry, the situation was so volatile that it could have erupted into extreme violence.

CHAPTER TWENTY-FOUR

Directly across the street from the Turner Avenue residence of the Fox family was the George Howland Elementary School. Its elementary education consisted of grades kindergarten through eighth. This was the mecca for education and recreation for most of the Fox grandchildren. The teachers were dedicated and disciplined, at times seemed a bit too strict, but determined to educate their charges.

The schoolyard was the center of activity for the entire neighborhood after school hours. Games of baseball and handball were the two sports engaged in by the boys, while the less strenuous sporting activities of rolling dice and playing cards filled the time of the older youths. The girls entertained themselves by jumping rope "double dutch," and hop-scotch. More mature young ladies stood around the perimeter of the yard, gossiping and admiring the aspiring young athletes. It was only the approaching darkness of the day that brought a halt to the activities. The demonstrative calls of anxious parents rang out from the houses across the street, reminding their offspring that it was bedtime.

Howland School was built in 1893 on the corner of 16th Street and Spaulding Avenue. It was built to meet the educational needs of the incoming immigrant children. In a relatively short period of time an addition was needed. Construction of the adjoining building was completed in 1913 and it spread to the alleyway on the south boundary of Spaulding Avenue. Near the end of World War I the flood gates of immigration were once more opened and Howland School found itself in need of still another addition to accommodate the influx. A third and final addition was built in 1925 on the corner of 16th Street and Turner Avenue.

With the impending birth of their fourth child, Bella and Philip were compelled once again to find larger living quarters. The lease on the apartment on Trumbull Avenue had just expired, so the opportunity to find a larger place to live was now at hand. They relocated to a new, more spacious apartment on 15th Street and Spaulding Avenue. Since the move was a short distance, they were able to continue to send their two older children, Edward and Esther, to Howland School.

On October 19, 1931, a second son, Myron, was born to Bella in Mt. Sinai hospital. Her two week stay, which was considered the normal recuperation period for a birth at that time, was highly welcomed, and much needed. But the anxiety she was experiencing, being away from her young children and home, did not let her fully enjoy her rest. Philip, during the two weeks of Bella's absence, was father and mother to the three children at home, and with the aid of his mother and sisters, he did a rather respectable job in the dual role.

Philip's steady income had been the family's weapon against the Depression. Because of this, when Myron was a year old, Philip felt compelled to return to the family building on Turner Avenue, in order to augment the family coffers again.

Thanks to the insurance and licensing regulations imposed by the city council, the taxi situation had calmed down as fewer unlicensed taxis appeared on the streets. Public transportation was proving again that it was the conveyance of choice amongst the masses. People walked longer and longer distances, however, in order to save the five cent fare. The smiles of the twenties had turned into the frowns of the thirties. Expressions of despair were becoming permanently etched in the faces of the new society of down and outers.

Although Philip was now considered part of management, his sympathies were still with the rank and file drivers. The strong union feelings that he had acquired as a journeyman plumber remained with him. The unions, continually trying to organize the drivers of Checker Cab, met with little success in the early 1930s. Most of the drivers were on a lease-operator agreement and they did not feel the need to belong to any collective organization.

After receiving the restoration of his full citizenship rights upon his release from prison, Philip once again was free to engage in one of his favorite pastimes: political debates. He expressed his point of view with great intensity and fire. He had become a devotee of Franklin Roosevelt, and at the mere mention of a negative view of his new political idol, Philip would immediately launch into a heated debate. On his lunch hour, Philip often would drive to the grounds of the Newberry Library, near downtown Chicago. It was this field opposite the library building that had the dubious name of "Bug House Square."

"Bug House Square" was a forum of free speech. Anyone of any political stripe, or with an opinion on any subject, was free to exercise his right to expound on his views. The more deliberate orators would carry with them a wooden box that had formerly been packed with bar soap as their platform. That would raise them above the crowd, and thus attract a larger audience. Every spokesperson, for good or evil, could be found here, elucidating his or her opinions and, more often than not, soliciting followers and dues paying members to his or her cause.

Philip would wander through the various knots of speakers and listeners and pause at the most anti-establishment and anti-government tirades and engage that speaker in a serious pro and con debate. Hunger and despair brought out the worst in people as they let their acrimony get the best of them. These lively discussions often turned into fist fights that had to be settled by the police, who were always on hand, just in case such an altercation erupted.

CHAPTER TWENTY-FIVE

It was great to be a Democrat in 1932, as the conventional wisdom held that anyone could beat Herbert Hoover. Philip was a loyal Democrat, and used a lot of his energy and his knowledge of Yiddish to register to vote a goodly number of immigrants who had recently attained their citizenship in the United States. The up-tempo tune of "Happy Days Are Here Again" was sung throughout the land as Franklin Delano Roosevelt swept into office in the landslide election in November 1932.

One month prior to the inauguration of President Roosevelt, in February of 1933, an assassination attempt was made in Miami, Florida, by an Italian immigrant named Giuseppe Zangara. The bullets that were fired in the direction of the President-elect missed him but hit several people next to him on the platform. Mayor Anton Cermak of Chicago, one of the dignitaries who was hit, was rushed to the hospital, mortally wounded. As he lay dying, with Roosevelt at his side, Mayor Cermak gathered enough strength to utter these words: "I am glad it was me, instead of you, Mr. President. The country needs you."

Indeed the country did need the new president. Immediately after his inauguration, President Roosevelt began implementing his programs to improve the economic and mental health of the nation. His first entreaty to the people to begin the healing process was this simple statement in his first Inaugural Address: "The only thing we have to fear, is fear itself."

Bella's preoccupation with the unglamorous portion of married life left her little time to worry about her family's life and conditions in Romania. But worry she did. The scourge of tuberculosis had found its way into the small town of Sulyetze in the eastern region of Romania. Two of Bella's siblings, a sister and a brother, developed this deadly disease and found themselves fighting for their lives. This tragedy occurred at a time before antibiotics, and a proven program for treatment had yet to be established. The older child, a girl named Sausse, was sent to a sanitarium in a large city in Romania to undergo whatever treatment was available. Her brother

Shapse was kept at home with his mother and sister and brothers until they could confirm that his malady was indeed tuberculosis.

Bella's earlier acquired frugality remained with her into her married life. She scrimped and saved whatever she could to accumulate a large enough kitty to send to her family in Romania. Her mother's eyesight was failing, and along with the worry and burden of her two ill children, she could not keep up with the demands that her occupation as a detail seamstress required. She was extremely grateful for the money she received from her loving, dutiful daughter in America. Within a short few months of the inception of the disease, word came to Chaya Frima that her daughter Sausse had passed away.

Bella received this devastating news about her younger sister in a tear streaked letter from her mother. Even though her own heart was breaking, Chaya Frima tried to console her oldest child through the written words of an anguished mother. Philip tried to ease the pain and sorrow, but Bella was left alone to carry out the Jewish mourning tradition of "shiva," seven long days of personal grief. Periods of crying and reflection did little to hasten the passing of this ancient ritual of sorrow. Mirrors, pictures and all measures of comfort and pleasure were avoided during this week of grief. Wooden boxes were substituted for couches and easy chairs, and shoes were not worn, to symbolize her loss. It was less than a year later when Bella's brother Shapse lost his battle to the tuberculin virus. He was just twenty-five years old. Bella had to repeat the mourning process, once again alone.

CHAPTER TWENTY-SIX

Chicago, along with the rest of the country, had run the range of experiences during the 1930s. It entered the decade with the hijinks of Prohibition, and all its accompanying accouterments: murder, shooting, prostitution, bribery and other corruption, followed by the devastation of the Depression. Chicago had its soup kitchens and bread lines, but it also had its bright lights.

The Chicago World's Fair of 1933 celebrated the 100th birthday of the city of Chicago, and was known as the "Century of Progress." It was an uplifting theme park built on the shores of beautiful Lake Michigan. The park employed hundreds of people, and generated much needed revenue for the city and its residents. Its ancillary effect spread over all phases of business. The final attendance figure for the Chicago World's Fair counted nearly thirty-nine million people filing through its turnstiles.

Chicago's Balaban and Katz theaters, for the sum of ten to fifteen cents a ticket, provided the release from life's ugly realities to the dream world of fantasy, adventure and comedy. For three hours, a patron was entertained with a double feature, cartoons and the latest news and sports results from around the world.

Chicago's notoriety as a gangster mecca did not diminish at all in the 1930s. The demise of John Dillinger, Public Enemy Number One, at the hands of FBI agents in July of 1934, did little to eradicate its lawless image. Baby Face Nelson, former partner of John Dillinger, met his end with seventeen slugs from the G-Men's guns in Niles, Illinois, just outside of Chicago. Al Capone had already been arrested in October of 1931, and sentenced to eleven years in prison for tax evasion. Even his incarceration did not alter the way the world viewed Chicago.

Labor strife and violence was the real "black-eye" of the United States in the 1930s, and Chicago was in the center of it, as usual. Union membership dwindled during the Depression and so did its collective power. Greedy and ruthless owners seized the opportunity once again to stifle the voice of the worker. They reduced wages, stopped improvements on working conditions and fired employees at will, with no just cause. The circle of violence was reborn. The owners hired "goons," and usually had the local police on their payroll. The workers carried baseball bats, guns, lead pipes and other paraphernalia of mayhem.

The camel's back was broken by a straw of injustice which occurred on Memorial Day of 1937. Outside the Republic Steel Plant in Chicago, a demonstration for better working conditions was taking place. The crowd was in a holiday mood, and the children were laughing and playing as they do at a picnic outing. It was not long before screams of pain and anguish permeated the air. One hundred and fifty police sailed into the crowd and attacked them with guns and night sticks and their notorious truncheons. The result of this quasi-official confrontation was ten dead and over 100 people injured. By the end of the decade, labor had won the war. Contracts were signed, conditions improved and union membership was back on the increase. Management also gained as productivity and profits rose, and company loyalty improved.

Amidst the labor turmoil of 1935, the taxi drivers once again tried to go against the owners and staged a huge rally in Grant Park along the shimmering shores of Lake Michigan. The drivers had formed a huge gathering of men and machines, and rhetoric and invectives filled the air. The professional agitators were on hand as usual, exhorting the drivers to defy the owners and go out on strike, even to the point of unlawfulness. The drivers were in a very nasty mood.

Philip was sent by his boss to observe the rally and report the troublemakers to him, so that he could take disciplinary action against them. This idea was repugnant to Philip, and he had decided on a course of action of his own. As he entered the perimeter of the angry gathering, he laid on the horn and started waving his arms side to side indicating to those directly in front of him to move their cars and let him through. When the drivers recognized Philip, they moved their cabs just enough to form a path to allow him to approach the center. Reaching the middle, he slammed down on the brakes, jumped out of the car and climbed on top of the hood. He borrowed a bull horn from one of the speakers, and began to enumerate the reasons why they were going about this protest in the wrong manner. He told the crowd that this was the worst possible time to call a work stoppage. The Depression was still strong in most areas in the country. Their families would be without food and shelter if the strike action lasted longer than a few weeks. He explained that they would accomplish a lot more by continuing to work, and entering into collective bargaining to air their grievances.

The longer Philip talked, the more convinced the drivers became. They trusted him, and his reputation as a square shooter went a long way to assuage their fears. Slowly the crowd dispersed, and the situation was diffused. Philip had accomplished what he thought was best for everyone.

During this period of labor conflict, Philip was kept busy troubleshooting isolated labor problems between drivers and management. He would attend drivers' rallies and placate most of their fears on the longevity of their occupation. His friendly demeanor made him particularly well-suited to this aspect of his job. One incident which occurred illustrates just how well-liked Philip had become. He made it part of his daily routine to check on the attendance and well-being of the various employees of the cab company who were working the main entrances to all of the hotels on Michigan Avenue.

He would start at the north end of this famous thoroughfare, stopping for a brief period of time at each hotel. All of the mounted policeman doing traffic duty on the street knew Philip, recognized his car and allowed him the necessary time to do his checking. On this particular day, Philip was driving a new car, and the officer on duty did not recognize it. He immediately began to write a parking ticket. The officer had just completed the citation when Philip emerged from the hotel. When the officer saw Philip and realized that it was his car, he became embarrassed. He expressed to Philip his regret, but explained that he could not destroy the ticket once it was written. In his attempt to receive Philip's forgiveness, the officer reached into his pocket and withdrew a five dollar bill, which he extended to Philip as payment for writing the ticket. With a huge grin of gratitude, Philip convinced his friend that the gesture was totally unnecessary and that he would pay the fine himself. Philip told the officer to use the fiver to buy his own kid a present.

The public relations portion of Philip's job reached its most fulfilling aspect right around the holiday season. It was his job to distribute hundreds of boxes of two-pound assorted chocolates to each and every switchboard operator, hotel doorman, and any person whose job it was to call a cab for a potential passenger.

As satisfying as it was to Philip at this time of the year to make people smile, it also was a great opportunity for his young sons to join him in giving away these holiday sweets. School was in recess for two weeks. The tradition of his sons' assistance was started with his son Edward and completed with his youngest son, Morton. As they approached each mounted police officer, Philip would pull alongside, and his son would hand a box of chocolates to the officer and then pet and talk to the officer's horse. This was a big thrill for a young city boy.

There were other forms of gifts for the special patrons and friends of the cab company: gift certificates from department stores and food certificates from large purveyors in Chicago. The glow of the season and the smiles and the thanks of the recipients always gave Phil a happy feeling.

CHAPTER TWENTY-SEVEN

1936 was a year of an emotional low for Bella. In the summer of that year, Bella once again suffered the trauma of loss. The news this time was even more devastating. She was informed by mail of the death of her mother. Chaya Frima's heart had given out. The loss of her two children at an early age, and her labors to make a living and a home for her family since the early death of her husband, proved to be too much for this struggling, courageous woman.

Bella could barely stand the pain. All of the old feelings of remorse, despair and especially the feeling that she had deserted her mother, that so filled her when she originally left Romania sixteen years ago, returned. Overwhelmed by these emotions, she once again had to observe the mourning ritual. Even with all of the love and affection from her husband and children, it was a very long time before Bella was to smile again.

During the last year of Max's life, 1937, an incident occurred in the bakery that would cause a bitter memory and would play heavily on the consideration of continuing the bakery operation after his death. The Bakers' Union, fighting for new members, had approached Max on several occasions to join them, along with his one baking assistant. Max felt that joining the organization would in no way benefit his worker or himself. He already was paying his assistant above scale plus additional benefits. This information he passed on to the overzealous organizers, interspersed with Yiddish epithets. This answer was not acceptable, and they began their campaign of harassment.

One Friday morning during the rush of business, two of the young hotheads from the Bakers Union heaved an odorous explosive missile, known in street parlance as a "stink bomb," into the crowded store front. The obnoxious smell drove away the customers, and then carried its repugnant scent into the baking area, contaminating all the products, and forcing Max and his assistant to vacate. This abomination of smell that so offended the nostrils permeated the air and rendered the bakery inoperable for several days.

When Philip and Jack were apprised of the situation, they became incensed and decided to allow Jack to negotiate with the union leadership. One evening during a union meeting at the Baker's Hall, Jack marched into the private office of the union president and demanded a hearing. The gentleman was taken aback, and wanted to know what was the nature of Jack's grievance. Jack removed his .32 caliber revolver from his pocket and while aiming it point blank at the startled and frightened union executive's head, he delivered his part of the negotiations. Jack stated to him in no uncertain terms, that if he or any member of his organization, ever committed another act of harassment against his father or his father's business, he personally would separate this union leader from his brain. Needless to say, the Fox family was never bothered again.

Max's life was laborious and troublesome, but also rewarding. In spite of the sometime chaotic experiences, he maintained the dignity of bearing and respect few people attain in their lifetime. He lived to see his family join him in America for a new beginning. He shepherded his children along the bumpy highway to young adulthood until they began raising their own families. The pride and joy he experienced in his grandchildren was the crown to his existence. Death took Max away from his beloved family on September 23, 1937. He was sixty-nine years old.

Up to the time of Max's death the bakery had been doing a fairly good business, although taking its physical toll on Max and Marion. Marion knew that in order to continue to run the bakery, she would need the stamina of one or both of her two sons. She offered the business to both of them, but each in turn declined to change occupations. Remembering his confrontation with the Bakers's Union, and now being busy with his electrical work, Jack turned down the offer from his mother. Philip also refused because he felt his position at the Checker Cab Company was secure and provided a substantial living for his family in these hard times. Fifty years of continuous baking had come to an end. Max and Marion had brought the baking business from Europe. The bakery never reopened following the funeral. The memories of the bakery remain in the minds of the older grandchildren even to this day, evoking happy thoughts and feelings.

In the cyclical nature of life a great loss is usually followed by a great joy. Max's passing was one of deep sorrow for his family, but the birth of Bella and Philip's last child, Morton, on July 28, 1938, eased the pain. Morton was a lovely, blond, curly-haired baby, and had the distinction of being the first male grandchild to be named after Max. It was the custom then, as it is still today, to bestow a Hebrew name upon the baby at the circumcision ritual. The new baby was given the name of Mordechai, in honor of his grandfather. It was a joyous occasion. The newest Fox infant forged a new link in the naming chain so important in Jewish history. Philip and Bella's family was now complete, three sons and two daughters.

CHAPTER TWENTY-EIGHT

1940 started the third cycle of the descendants of Max and Marion. Things were changing. Turner Avenue had been renamed Christiana Avenue in the mid-1930s. The bakery was now closed and history.

The war in Europe was reverberating in the United States, and a case of war nerves was surfacing throughout the land. Most heavy industrial plants were beginning to convert to military tooling. Parts for automobiles were becoming scarce and affecting the taxi industry as well as the driving public. New vehicle production had come to a halt; consequently the old cabs were starting to fall apart and becoming unroadworthy and unsafe for the drivers and passengers. Philip's job had taken on an additional function. Along with his other duties, he had to keep track of these crippled and unsafe vehicles. He recorded their vehicle numbers and informed the maintenance garages and drivers that the condition of their vehicles was unsafe and repairs were to be made immediately. As gas rationing set in later on, he also had to enforce the distance restrictions placed on the taxi industry.

It was a difficult rule to enforce, because to enforce it meant a great loss of revenue to the drivers. The boundaries were the Chicago city limits. Even the next door suburbs were out of bounds. On a Saturday afternoon in May of 1943, Philip had positioned himself outside the main gate at one of the city of Cicero's race tracks. He was to list all of the cab vehicle numbers arriving and discharging passengers. The race tracks were but a scant few blocks from the Chicago city boundary. As the cabs kept up a steady stream of arrivals, Philip assigned the duty of recording the numbers to his middle son, Myron. Philip continued to observe all of the happenings around him. As time passed, the list got longer and longer.

By the end of the afternoon, when the last of the horse players departed, Philip turned to his son and requested the list of numbers he had compiled. He looked at the paper and contemplated all the numbers for a long time. Finally he took the paper in both hands and shredded it to pieces. He knew that if he turned in this list, a couple of hundred drivers could possibly lose their jobs. His concern for their welfare would not allow him do it.

Once Congress approved the first peace time draft in late 1940, apprehension and worry was an everyday concern for all families with eligible young men of draft age. The Fox family had several grandsons who fit this category. Anticipation of the call up was enough to drive the women to tears.

On December 7, 1941, a lightning bolt struck the nation. Japan had launched its sneak attack on Pearl Harbor that fateful Sunday. The electrical charge produced by that lightning had carried over into December 8th. The country was still in shock and considering all of the consequences of that dastardly act. That day, in an address to a joint session of Congress, President Roosevelt answered the Japanese action with a declaration of war.

Three days later, on December 11th, Italy and Germany declared war on the United States. The country's previous attitude of isolationism had taken a 180 degree turn. Patriotism soared and a united country cranked up the war effort to fever pitch. The common goal of total victory was the battle cry that rallied the people for the next four and one-half years.

The first of the grandsons to be called up was Abe Kreiter. On December 4, 1941, he boarded a slow train, bound for his basic training. All draftees aboard were to serve in this peace time call-up for one year. On December 7th, while still on the train, the news of the Japanese attack on Pearl Harbor spread through the cars like wildfire. A great hush fell over the entire train, in contrast to the noisy camaraderie that existed just a few short moments earlier. Each new draftee sank back into his own thoughts as he tried to sort out all of the ramifications of this tragic news. In just one short day, they learned that their one year status had been changed to one of "the duration plus."

Patriotism was not lost on Philip Fox. Right after the declaration of war was announced, the government came out with a program known as "Civil Defense." This program was created to prepare and inform the populace about any possible invasions or bombing raids by our enemies. Philip immediately volunteered his services to the program. The larger metropolitan areas were divided into zones, and then fragmented into square block sections. He became assistant zone warden and block captain of his unit.

The primary duty of the Civil Defense workers was to be prepared for any contingencies that might arise. They were to be alert to any signs of sabotage, or subversive activities; watch the night skies for unusual plane movements; and lead the local population into action in support of the war effort. Assemblies and meetings were held once a month in each unit. The latest allowable information from the government was disseminated, and often a featured speaker was present to inform the people as well.

Each block meeting was opened with the "Pledge of Allegiance" to the flag and then followed by a rendition of the "Star Spangled Banner." At age three and one-half years, Philip's youngest child, Morton, stood on a tall platform and led the recitation of the Pledge. The audience responded in kind, as patriotism had no age limits. Everyone understood that rationing was essential, although inconvenient. Collecting scrap metal, paper, and even cooking grease became vital to the war effort. Howland School became the central collection point for these important ingredients in the manufacture of war materiel.

Philip built and installed a bulletin board alongside the tall flag pole in front of the family building on Christiana Avenue. The flag was raised every morning and lowered every evening, dutifully accompanied by a snappy salute. He used the bulletin board as an open central point of communication for the neighbors. He posted recent photos of all of the young men from the neighborhood serving in the Armed Forces, bulletins from the government, and any newspaper clippings of important events and personal items about the local young warriors of the neighborhood. He always made himself available to any people with problems. If he could not help them himself with advice, he would then direct them to the proper authorities, or to others who could.

In the early months of the war, rumors of suspected subversives were heard everywhere, 99% not true, but every once in a while a rumor turned into a tentative lead, and finally a trial and conviction. Such an incident occurred in Philip's block involving the building on Christiana Avenue. One noon hour in April of 1942, when the children came home for lunch, they noticed two strange gentlemen in the basement of the building. They inquired of their mother as to who they were and what they were doing there? Bella answered rather curtly that they were from the telephone company and were checking out a reported problem on the phone line.

During that particular phase of the telephonic evolution, telephones did not have the privacy that we enjoy and appreciate today. Everyone was on a party line, and interruptions of conversations were a common occurrence. The telephone lines ran down the full length of the alley, from one intersection to the next. At the far end of the alley, at Ogden Avenue, was a bakery, which had been located there for several years. The owners were of German descent. According to the story that was revealed following the war, the adult members of this family joined the German-American Bund prior to America's involvement in the Second World War. Their sympathies and support for Hitler and the Nazi government grew stronger with each passing day.

In this predominately Jewish neighborhood, it was unusual to have neighbors of another ethnic background. However, they were scattered throughout the neighborhood and generally, they were affable and friendly, and welcomed the incoming Jewish families. However, the outbreak of war brought forth the true feelings of some of them. There was no sitting on the fence. The war tested the Americanization of the immigrants, no matter how long they had been here. The German-American Bund had been preparing for this moment for a long time. Their propaganda machinery had been feeding the early Nazi sympathizers the party line for several years uninterruptedly.

It was apparent to the FBI early in the war that among the true believers in this Nazi verbiage was the family from the bakery. They became active participants not only in the Nazi thought process, but they decided to go even further and engage in espionage and sabotage on behalf of Germany. Their bakery, which consisted of three ovens, had been set up for this purpose. One was used for baking, while the other two had been devised for a short wave radio and the storage of arms and munitions. They had been under surveillance for a period before the war broke out. They had been discovered through a tip, and had now become the focus of an FBI investigation. The undercover agent most responsible for their final apprehension and conviction was the principal of Howland School, Mr. H.R. Liddil.

The two gentlemen purportedly from the telephone company, who had been occupying the basement on Christiana Avenue, were actually FBI agents. Recording the phone conversations of these subversives, they were able to compile huge amounts of evidence and proof of their complicity in this plot against the United States. Philip and Bella meanwhile maintained their discreet silence, while seeing to the comfort and needs of these agents. They remained about a week until they concluded their portion of the undercover investigation. Nothing further was known about this incident until after the war, when an assembly was held in the Howland School auditorium honoring the principal, Mr. Liddil, for his part in the investigation. The owner of the bakery and his oldest son were found guilty of treason and sentenced to a federal penitentiary to serve out their terms.

CHAPTER TWENTY-NINE

"D" Day, June 6, 1944, was the beginning of the end for the Axis armies in Europe. The Allies had finally launched the invasion on the belly of Europe. The second front began and the crush from east and west was too much for the German Army. Other than their last ditch attempt at a counter-offensive at the Battle of the Bulge in Belgium, the entire German Army was retreating in disarray and just a few short months later the war in Europe was over. "VE" Day on May 8, 1945, brought a huge sigh of relief to the country, while the American people still maintained a watchful eye on the other side of the world. The Japanese had not given any hint of a desire to surrender and to the contrary had sworn to defend their islands to the end.

But the cessation of hostilities in Europe gave America the opportunity for a breather it so desperately needed. Philip and Bella and the entire Fox clan celebrated with all Chicagoans and the rest of the country. They prayed that their son Edward and their nephews assigned to the European theatre would finally be out of harm's way.

June 6th also had a melancholy significance for Philip and Bella and the children. When the news broke about the invasion, they were in the midst of moving. The building had been sold a few years earlier, and the new owners now required the apartment for their own use. The long chain of association with this four flat residence was rapidly coming to a close. Twenty-two years in this habitat had witnessed the marriages of the sons and daughters of Max and Marion and the birth of most of their grandchildren. All of the good times, bad times and sad times they had shared together here would become a nostalgic memory to be recalled often in the future. They were not moving very far, but to the children it seemed worlds away.

In August of 1945, two atomic bombs were released over Japan. The first was exploded over Hiroshima and the next over Nagasaki. Japan had been brought to submission, and surrendered unconditionally to her victors. The Second World War was over at last. August 14, 1945, was a day for which the world had been longing.

The boys came marching home, and among those returning warriors were Max and Marion's grandsons, who had left to serve their country several years earlier. Each returned home with a huge smile on his face that told of his gladness to be back, but also etched with the lines of weariness that were produced by the days and months and years of active service. Jubilation rang out as the families welcomed home their loved ones.

CHAPTER THIRTY

Glad that the war was over, and his son and nephews safely home, Philip took the time to step back and reflect on the past years of his life: how his fortunes had been so tied to those of the cab company, his loyalty to them and the early struggles he had survived. He now concluded he had reached a dead end in his future with them. His boss, Mike Sokol, was looking to infuse young and new personnel into the company. Trying to change the former image of the Checker Cab Company, he was offering any and all deals to the old-timers to induce them to leave. Attrition was not working fast enough to suit him. Philip was ready for a change, and when Mike Sokol offered him a goodly sum to leave, he accepted it, and once and for all shut the door on the early and middle years of his life. He realized how different his life would have been were it not for his faith in God, the love and support of his wife and family, and all the people who believed in him. Those early bitter chapters in his life were now closed, and never to be looked upon again by him.

EPILOGUE

Philip Fox spent the rest of his life totally devoted to his family, while returning to the religiosity that so dominated the lives of his mother and father. After leaving the cab company, he purchased a small business in partnership with his uncle. The tuxedo rental business they acquired was a long established company, located in the Chicago "Loop," on the corner of Dearborn and Randolph Streets. The clientele consisted of musicians and entertainers appearing in the downtown clubs and theatres, and also persons who attended weddings and proms throughout the Midwest. Both being novices as entrepreneurs, they committed the cardinal sin of being too trusting of the person from whom they purchased the business. The paper work had been completed and the deal had been concluded on a Friday afternoon, but neglected in the process was the taking of a certified inventory.

When Philip and his uncle arrived Monday morning to take over the business, they discovered to their total dismay that the inventory had been switched, and that all the new and up-to-date tuxedos had been removed and replaced with worn and outdated garments. They were heartbroken, but realized they had been had by a scheming, dishonest shark. Once again, Philip's trust in his fellow man had done him in. And like most small businesses following World War II, they were caught in the squeeze of the growing local and national chains, and along with the costly process of updating the inventory, they were forced to close their doors after a relatively short period. But true to his own impeccable tastes, Philip liked the men's clothing business and decided to stay with it. He remained in men's apparel until he reached retirement age.

When he was informed that he had to retire at age sixty-five because the owner considered him too old to perform his sales duties, Philip engaged in his final battle for worker equality. His fellow workers at his establishment acknowledged his abilities and were shocked at the action of the owner. Philip, as a member of the Retail Clerks Union, took his private war to the local union business agent. The business agent looked upon this problem as a personal affront as his age was approaching eighty. Between the two of them, and after several meetings with the owner, they were able to convince him of the folly of his thinking and thus worked out an equitable agreement. Philip did not want to continue his employment there and thus was well compensated instead.

His devoted nephews, the sons of his sister and brother-in-law, Pauline and Sam Kreiter, offered him a position with their printing supply business. He eagerly accepted, and worked devotedly for the next ten years. Finally at age seventy-five, he decided it was time to retire. His grandchildren were the lights of his life. He and his wife Bella spent as much time with their youngest progeny as possible. The balance of his years on earth were quality time in good health. He attended synagogue services nearly every day at Congregation B'nai Jacob of Rogers Park, 6200 N. Artesian Avenue, weather permitting, and continued his self-education with books of all types, but primarily those of an historical nature. Throughout his life, Philip gained the respect of everyone who made his acquaintance, and retained in full fervor the love of his family.

In his lifetime, Philip never impugned the judicial system, which in his early years aided and abetted in his unjust incarceration. He never gave up on the system, even in prison. He knew that the American system of laws that he lived under were still the best in the world, and would eventually right the wrong that was done to him. Three years later it did. He always preached the love of and devotion to his adopted country to his children and grandchildren. Respect he earned and respect he maintained. Philip Fox passed away June 24, 1982.

Bella lived to celebrate her ninety-second birthday May 14, 1997, surrounded by her loving children, grandchildren, great-grandchildren, and great-great-grandchildren, nephews, nieces and friends. She remained sharp of mind and quick-witted, and developed an aged beauty that had evolved from her earlier comeliness. She maintained her own apartment and was the senior resident of an apartment building set aside for older occupants. Her common sense approach to life was still one of the great attributes she possessed. She passed away on November 3, 1997.

Bella's worry and concern for her brothers and sisters during the Nazi occupation, and then the Communist regime in Romania, were finally allayed. All of her family emigrated to Israel in the late 1950s and early 1960s, and then two years prior to the Six Day War between Israel and her Arab neighbors, Bella embarked on one of the most joyous journeys in her life. Along with her husband Philip, she left on a trip to Israel and a reunion with her family, for the first time in forty-five years. They landed at the airport outside of Tel-Aviv amid a small sea of flowers and tears of joy.

The years of anxiety and worry melted away as she caressed the faces of her beloved siblings. The shock of seeing them as middle-aged adults, while remembering them as children, was soon past, and the present was all that mattered. It was a glorious reunion, and during the next several years, Bella and Philip were able to enjoy two more lengthy trips back to Israel and her family.

She continued to be the guiding light and inspiration to her entire family. She was the last remaining generational member of her family and her husband Philip's family as well.

Marion, the matriarch of the family, died in Chicago on February 5, 1958, at the age of eighty-five years. Short on formal education, but long on fortitude and grit, she held tenaciously to her position in life as mother, teacher and advisor to her children and grandchildren, almost to the very end. Her charitable and religious way of life remained in the forefront of her later years, and she continued to receive the adoration of the religious community around her. Until her death in 1958, Marion maintained her place of honor at all family weddings, bar mitzvahs and ritual circumcisions. She was the rock through troubled times who never let down in the face of adversity. Her resolute determination was passed down to her children and grandchildren.

In the research and writing of this story, most of the secrets from the past were revealed to us. However, there is one mystery that will always remain. This is the strained relationship between the Fox brothers, Philip and Jack. It is a classic story. Something must have transpired in their early youth to trigger this strange fraternal phenomenon. For as long as the children can remember, Philip and

Jack never spoke directly to each other. They loved each other, they protected each other and they expressed great concern for each other's welfare, but only addressed one another through a third person.

On the occasions when Jack and Faye attended Sabbath meals at Philip and Bella's home, it would be a happy time with the young children around the food-laden table. The conversation would be light and airy, and then it would happen. Jack would ask through a third person at the table for Philip to pass the condiments. After a brief period of time, the situation would be reversed. It seems regrettable now after so many years that no one ever bothered to ask why. We have now come to the only possible conclusion, that this strange conversational conduct between them stemmed from the early troubles they encountered in the taxi industry.

Jack and Faye were never able to conceive children of their own. Faye often expressed her personal grief at their inability to produce an offspring. Despite encouragement from his family to adopt children, Jack remained strenuously opposed. Instead, he reveled in the love shown to him by his nieces and nephews. In his later years, his gruff exterior and blunt manner often hid his deep emotions and affection for the children of his brother and sisters.

From the end of 1945 until the completion of this book, all the family of Max and Marion Fox, their children and their spouses, have passed away. With their passing, Pauline and Sam Kreiter, Fanny and Sam Geltner, Philip and Bella Fox, Jack and Faye Fox, Bertha and Morris Hyman and Rose and Maurice Halap closed the chapter on the vibrant immigrant generation of the family.

Today there is an ongoing debate as to who our role models should be. Who are the people that our children should look up to and emulate? The list runs the gamut from athletic superstars to the outrageous rock and roll personalities, and the stars of the entertainment world in general.

This superficial list is thin at best. The search for the true heroes and role models does not go deep enough or far enough. To really find the person who is head and shoulders above the rest, to fill this deserving niche in our lives, we must seek within our family unit first, for in our familial structure, we will always find the person or persons who are more deserving of our praise and adoration than the other artificial icons vying for the role.

Whether early on or later in life, we will eventually recognize that it is our parents or grandparents or other relatives close to us who have shown the courage and fortitude to survive and strive to move forward under trying times and the worst of conditions.

Philip and Bella Fox met all the requirements for this place of honor. Throughout their lives they taught their children integrity, honesty and diligence in the face of adversity. They also showed by example their patriotism and esteem for their adopted land, in spite of the flaws that American society exhibits, both then and now. But their greatest lesson is the one of love. Their quiet devotion and affection for each other set a strong and everlasting pattern for their children to follow.

■

ABOUT THE AUTHOR

Myron H. Fox was born at Mount Sinai Hospital in Chicago in 1931. He attended the George Howland Elementary School and the David Farragut High School, both on the West Side, and received his GED High School Equivalency diploma while serving in the military.

He served for four years in the United States Air Force, from October 1950 to October 1954, including one year in Korea in 1953-54. He had attained the rank of Airman First Class (equivalent to sergeant) at the time of his honorable discharge.

Mr. Fox has had a broad range of experience, including stints as a union ironworker for six years; manager of a retail floor covering business for ten years; and partner for eighteen years including president for fourteen years of a company which manufactured hair care products. In 1993, he sold the business and retired.

In May, 1948, he was the winner of an essay contest sponsored by United Airlines and the Chicago Board of Education. The topic was: *The Thirtieth Year Anniversary of Air Mail.* This whetted his appetite for historical writing. He is currently working on several short stories and other pieces.

Mr. Fox was married in 1950 to Frances Louise Rosenburg. They have seven children, four daughters and three sons; and nine grandchildren, eight girls and one boy.

■

THE DORIS MINSKY MEMORIAL FUND SPONSORS

The following sponsors, by their generous donations, have made possible the creation of the Doris Minsky Memorial Fund and this publication.

Leah and Leslie Axelrod
American Jewish Congress
Mr. and Mrs. Lester Bachmann
Steve Barnett
Lawrence D. Bastone
Merrily and David Birkenstein
Sylvia J. Boecker
Bureau on Jewish Employment Problems
Jules E. Coven
Dr. and Mrs. Irving H. Cutler
Fred Eychaner
Judith and Terry Feiertag
Etha Beatrice Fox
Gary C. Furin
Mr. and Mrs. Gilbert Gavlin
Mr. and Mrs. Harry Gee, Jr.
Mr. and Mrs. Charles A. Giulini, Jr.
Carolyn B. Haas
Mr. and Mrs. Craig R. Hoffheimer
Shirley and Sol Leavitt
Milton and Iona Levenfeld
Larry and Beth Levine
Robert B. Lifton
Jerome and Paula Mandell
Mark Mandle
The Hon. Abraham Lincoln Marovitz

Elihu and Matilda Massel
Mr. and Mrs. Hyman Minsky
Jeremy Michael Minsky
Joseph Minsky
Laurence Minsky
Sarah Louise Minsky
Stuart and Julie Minsky
Steve and Peggy McCormick
Sam and Janice Roberman
Sidney Robin
Ethel Rochlin
Sam Rochlin
Jonah Rosenberg
Marion and Earl Rosenstein
Walter Roth
Joyce and Harold Saffir
Moselle A. Schwartz
Norman D. Schwartz
Frieda and Arnold Shure
Joseph P. Shure
Gary Matthew Spraker
Barbara A. Susman
Gabriel Videla
Widman, Goldberg & Zulkie, Ltd.
Mae Yonemura
Marlene and Leonard Zekman
  and Family

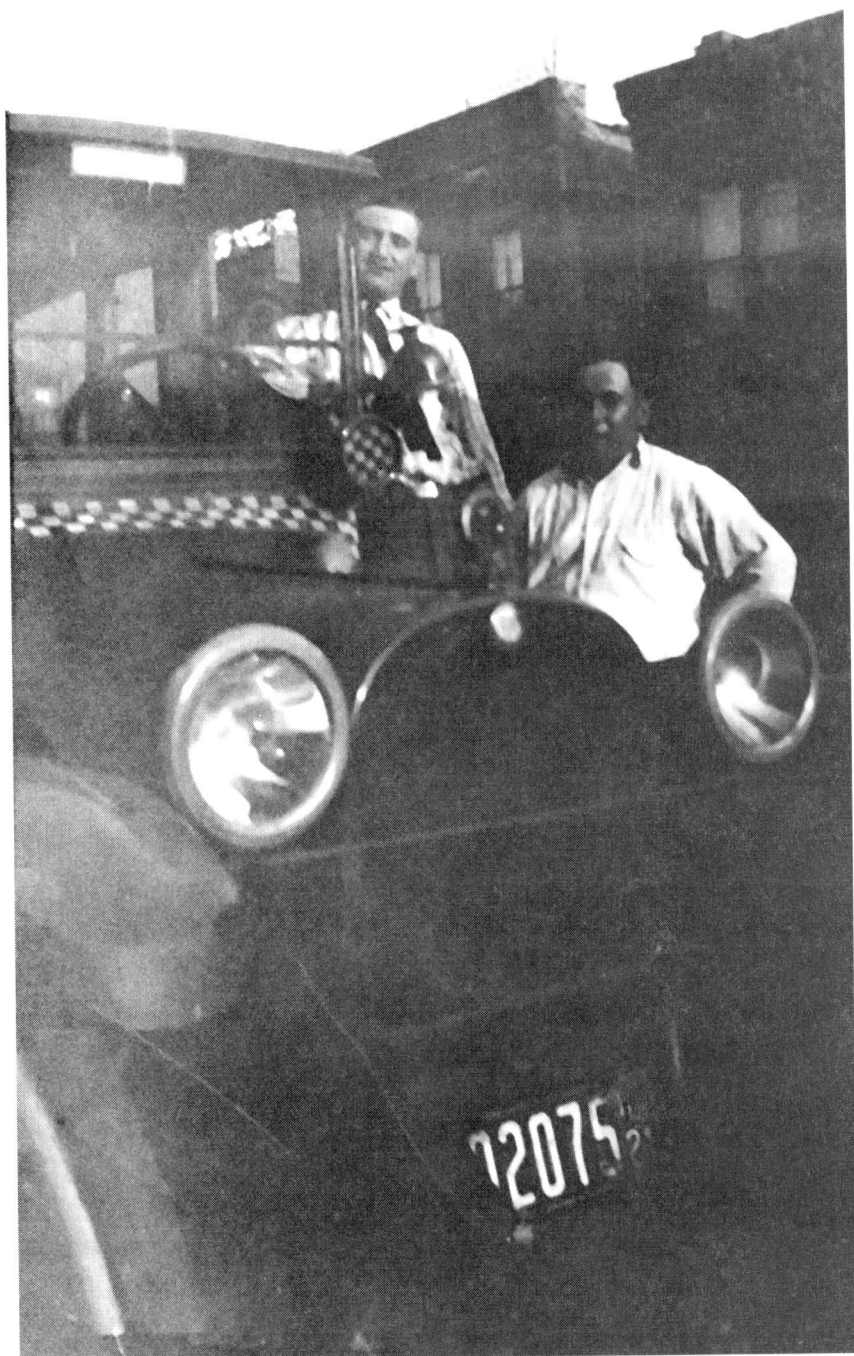

Philip Fox (left) with his taxicab in 1921. (From collection of Myron H. Fox)

Northwest corner of Kedzie Avenue and Roosevelt Road, the site of shooting as of 1998. View is from east to west. Shooting occurred at taxicab stand, located where the bushes are. Roosevelt Road is out of view to left. (Photograph by Myron H. Fox.)

Four-story red brick building is site of David J. Brown's restaurant, 2002 W. Division Street, located on southeast corner of Damen Avenue and Division Street, as of 1998. Damen goes north and south (left and right in photograph). Automobiles going to and from viewer are on Division Street, going east and west. Empty lot to right of building was site of Brown's pool hall; the guns were found in the alley in back of the pool hall. (Photograph by Myron H. Fox.)

Fox family in 1932, before birth of youngest child, Morton. Top row: Philip and Bella; Middle row: Myron and Edward; Bottom row: Helen and Esther. (From collection of Myron H. Fox)

Building to right with scaffolding is 1618 S. Christiana Avenue (formerly 1618 S. Turner Avenue), residence of the Fox family for many years, as of 1998. (Photograph by Myron H. Fox.)

Original building of the Howland School, southwest corner, 16th Street and Spaulding Avenue, as of 1998. Spaulding is to left, running north and south. 16th Street is to right, running east and west. (Photograph by Myron H. Fox.)